C000165147

SIDE DISH

RECIPES

Enjoy Everyday With Easy Potato Side Dish Cookbook!

(An Inspiring Side Dish Casserole Cookbook for You)

Rhonda Benn

Published by Alex Howard

Side Dish Recipes: Enjoy Everyday With Easy Potato Side Dish Cookbook!
(An Inspiring Side Dish Casserole Cookbook for You)

ISBN 978-1-990169-64-9

Legal & Disclaimer

The information contained in this book is not designed to replace or take the place of any form of medicine or professional medical advice. The information in this book has been provided for educational and entertainment purposes only.

Table of contents

Part 1

Air Fryer Baked Potatoes

"Beautifully crusty on the outside and light and fluffy on the inside, just like a great baked potato should be! Serve them with your favorite topping, like sour cream, butter, or chives."

Serving: 2 | Prep: 5 m | Cook: 1 h | Ready in: 1 h 5 m

Ingredients

- 2 large russet potatoes, scrubbed
- 1 tablespoon peanut oil
- 1/2 teaspoon coarse sea salt

Direction

- Preheat air fryer to 400 degrees F (200 degrees C).
- Brush potatoes with peanut oil and sprinkle with salt. Place them in the air fryer basket and place basket in the air fryer.
- Cook potatoes until done, about 1 hour. Test for doneness by piercing them with a fork.

Nutrition Information

- Calories: 344 calories
- Total Fat: 7.1 g

- Cholesterol: 0 mg
- Sodium: 462 mg
- Total Carbohydrate: 64.5 g
- Protein: 7.5 g

Air Fryer Sweet Potato Tots

"These sweet potato tots have a kick, and are made lighter by preparing them in the air fryer. Serve with ketchup or your favorite dipping sauce."

Serving: 24 | Prep: 15 m | Cook: 35 m | Ready in: 1 h

Ingredients

- 2 sweet potatoes, peeled
- 1/2 teaspoon Cajun seasoning
- olive oil cooking spray
- sea salt to taste

Direction

- Bring a pot of water to a boil and add sweet potatoes. Boil until potatoes can be pierced with a fork but are still firm, about 15 minutes. Do not over-boil, or they will be messy to grate. Drain and let cool.
- Grate sweet potatoes into a bowl using a box grater. Carefully mix in Cajun seasoning. Form mixture into tot-shaped cylinders.
- Spray the air fryer basket with olive oil spray. Place tots in the basket in a single row without touching each other or the

sides of the basket. Spray tots with olive oil spray and sprinkle with sea salt.

- Heat air fryer to 400 degrees F (200 degrees C) and cook tots for 8 minutes. Turn, spray with more olive oil spray, and sprinkle with more sea salt. Cook for 8 minutes more.

Nutrition Information

- Calories: 21 calories
- Total Fat: 0 g
- Cholesterol: 0 mg
- Sodium: 36 mg
- Total Carbohydrate: 4.8 g
- Protein: 0.4 g

Amazing Oven Roasted Potatoes

"With these potatoes, you wont miss the loads of oil in regular fried potatoes. Golden on the outside, tender on the inside."

Serving: 6 | Prep: 10 m | Cook: 1 h | Ready in: 1 h 10 m

Ingredients
- 6 potatoes, cut into chunks
- 2 tablespoons olive oil
- 1 teaspoon seasoned salt
- 1 teaspoon salt
- 1 teaspoon cracked black pepper

Direction
- Preheat oven to 400 degrees F (200 degrees C).
- Rinse and dry potatoes with a paper towel and transfer to a large bowl. Add olive oil, seasoned salt, salt, and black pepper; mix well. Spread potatoes on a baking sheet.
- Bake in preheated oven for 30 minutes, turning potatoes occasionally. Continue baking until potatoes are tender and golden brown, about 30 minutes more.

Nutrition Information
- Calories: 205 calories
- Total Fat: 4.7 g
- Cholesterol: 0 mg

- Sodium: 554 mg
- Total Carbohydrate: 37.6 g
- Protein: 4.4 g

ApplePear Sauce

"This is a great flavor in time for the holidays. Perfectly paired Red Delicious and Asian pears make for a great twist on your traditional apple sauce."

Serving: 12 | Prep: 15 m | Cook: 35 m | Ready in: 50 m

Ingredients

- 6 Red Delicious apples - peeled, cored, and cut into cubes
- 4 Asian pears - peeled, cored, and cut into cubes
- 1/2 cup apple cider
- 2 tablespoons white sugar
- 2 tablespoons ground cinnamon

Direction

- Heat a large skillet over medium-high heat. Stir apples, Asian pears, and apple cider together in the skillet until the fruit is mushy, about 10 minutes.
- Smash the apples and pears with the back of a wooden spoon until no large chunks remain; continue cooking until thickened, 20 to 30 minutes more.
- Stir sugar and cinnamon into the sauce; cook, stirring occasionally, until the sugar dissolves completely, 5 to 7 minutes more.

Nutrition Information
- Calories: 69 calories
- Total Fat: 0.2 g
- Cholesterol: 0 mg
- Sodium: 2 mg
- Total Carbohydrate: 18.2 g
- Protein: 0.4 g

Auntie Marys Sweet Potato Fritters

"My Aunt made this for my friends and me as an after-school snack. It's savory and sweet at the same time. With sweet potatoes and carrots, these will make you smile. Serve with sour cream."

Serving: 10 | Prep: 15 m | Cook: 2 m | Ready in: 22 m

Ingredients
- 4 sweet potatoes, shredded
- 3 large carrots, shredded
- 1/2 cup vegetable oil
- salt and ground black pepper to taste

Direction
- Mix sweet potatoes and carrots together in a large bowl. Form into small balls and flatten into patties.
- Heat oil in a large skillet over medium-high heat. Fry patties in hot oil until golden brown, about 1 minute per side. Drain on paper towels; allow to cool slightly, about 5 minutes. Season with salt and pepper.

Nutrition Information
- Calories: 116 calories
- Total Fat: 1.2 g
- Cholesterol: 0 mg
- Sodium: 93 mg
- Total Carbohydrate: 24.9 g
- Protein: 2 g

Awesome Smashed Red Potatoes

"This recipe of hand-mashed red potatoes with skins with a flavor mixture of bacon bits, cheese, and French onion rings could be served as a main dish if you are a potato-lover like me. This is the only way my family will allow me to serve potatoes in our house. The amounts I have suggested are only guidelines; you will adjust these over time to your taste."

Serving: 4 | Prep: 15 m | Cook: 20 m | Ready in: 35 m

Ingredients
- 4 large red potatoes, cut into 8 wedges
- 3/4 cup sliced processed cheese food (such as Velveeta®)
- 2/3 cup crushed French-fried onions (such as French's®)
- 1/3 cup bacon bits (such as Hormel®)
- 2 tablespoons milk, or as needed

Direction
- Place potatoes into a pot and cover with water; bring to a boil. Reduce heat to medium-low and simmer until tender, about 20 minutes; drain.
- Mix processed cheese, French-fried onions, bacon bits into potatoes and smash together using a potato masher. Stir milk into potatoes, increasing amount until desired consistency is reached.

Nutrition Information
- Calories: 645 calories
- Total Fat: 29.7 g
- Cholesterol: 34 mg
- Sodium: 1057 mg
- Total Carbohydrate: 77.6 g
- Protein: 17.3 g

Bacon Apples

"I cooked apples that I stuffed with brown sugar and cinnamon over a campfire as a dessert for my family when we went camping. In the morning we had bacon with our breakfasts and the kids marinated the bacon in the leftover apples! The bacon was good but we ate the apples after and they where surprisingly good!"

Serving: 2 | Prep: 10 m | Cook: 8 m | Ready in: 18 m

Ingredients
- 2 apples, cored
- 1/4 cup brown sugar
- 1 teaspoon ground cinnamon, or more to taste
- 4 slices cooked bacon, crumbled

Direction

- Build a campfire and allow the fire to burn until it has accumulated a bed of coals. Rake the coals into a flat bed on one side of the fire. Alternatively, preheat an outdoor grill.
- Place apples in a loaf pan. Combine brown sugar and cinnamon in a bowl; spoon into each apple.
- Place the loaf pan into the campfire or on the grill; cook for about 3 minutes. Carefully remove the pan from the fire and sprinkle bacon over apples. Place in the fire or on the grill for about 5 minutes more.

Nutrition Information
- Calories: 244 calories
- Total Fat: 5.3 g
- Cholesterol: 13 mg
- Sodium: 286 mg
- Total Carbohydrate: 47.1 g
- Protein: 4.9 g

Bacon Home Fries

"Diced potatoes, peppers, and onions cooked in bacon drippings."

Serving: 4 | Prep: 15 m | Cook: 25 m | Ready in: 40 m

Ingredients
- 1/2 pound bacon
- 4 potatoes, diced
- 1 small onion, diced
- 1 green bell pepper, diced
- salt and ground black pepper to taste

Direction
- Place the bacon in a large skillet and cook over medium-high heat, turning occasionally, until evenly browned, about 10 minutes. Let bacon cool on a plate lined with paper towel.
- Drain all but 2 tablespoons fat from the skillet. Stir potatoes, onion, and bell pepper into reserved drippings; season with salt and pepper and cook, stirring every 3 to 4 minutes and pressing the potatoes with the back of a spatula, until potatoes are golden brown and soft, 15 to 20 minutes. Crumble bacon over the potato mixture and stir.

Nutrition Information
- Calories: 277 calories
- Total Fat: 8 g
- Cholesterol: 20 mg
- Sodium: 480 mg
- Total Carbohydrate: 40.5 g
- Protein: 11.6 g

BaconGarlic Green Beans

"Another family favorite vegetable side-dish that is simple and quick to make. Great for family dinners, Thanksgiving, or any occasion. You can substitute lime zest for the lemon zest, if desired."

Serving: 12 | Prep: 15 m | Cook: 20 m | Ready in: 35 m

Ingredients
- 3 pounds fresh green beans, trimmed
- 4 slices bacon
- 1 cup butter
- 4 cloves garlic, minced
- 1/2 teaspoon lemon zest

Direction

- Place green beans in a pot and cover with water; bring to a boil. Reduce heat to medium-low and simmer until beans start to soften, about 10 minutes. Drain water, leaving beans in the pot.
- Place bacon strips on a microwave-safe plate and cook in the microwave until crisp, about 2 minutes. Cool and crumble bacon.
- Stir butter and bacon into beans in the pot and return to medium heat; cook and stir until butter melts, 2 to 3 minutes. Add garlic; cook and stir until fragrant, 3 to 4 minutes. Top with lemon zest and stir.

Nutrition Information

- Calories: 189 calories
- Total Fat: 16.7 g
- Cholesterol: 44 mg
- Sodium: 185 mg

- Total Carbohydrate: 8.5 g
- Protein: 3.4 g

Baked Asparagus with Portobello Mushrooms and Thyme

"Asparagus and portobello mushroom work great together, especially when baked in the oven. You can use any herbs you like, but our family loves thyme."

Serving: 4 | Prep: 10 m | Cook: 15 m | Ready in: 25 m

Ingredients
- 2 pounds fresh asparagus, trimmed
- 2 portobello mushroom caps, cut into strips
- 2 tablespoons olive oil
- 3 sprigs fresh thyme, leaves removed
- salt and freshly ground black pepper

Direction

- Preheat the oven to 450 degrees F (230 degrees C). Lightly grease a baking sheet.
- Combine asparagus and portobello mushrooms in a bowl and drizzle with olive oil. Season with thyme, salt, and pepper. Mix well to combine. Spread in one layer on the prepared baking sheet.
- Bake in the preheated oven until asparagus is tender, about 8 minutes. Turn and bake for an additional 8 to 12 minutes, depending on the thickness of asparagus spears. Season with salt and pepper.

Nutrition Information
- Calories: 109 calories
- Total Fat: 7.1 g
- Cholesterol: 0 mg
- Sodium: 44 mg
- Total Carbohydrate: 9.6 g

- Protein: 5.4 g

Baked Corn on the Cob

"For great corn on the cob indoors."

Serving: 2 | Prep: 5 m | Cook: 1 h | Ready in: 2 h 5 m

Ingredients
- 1 quart water, or as needed
- 1/2 cup white sugar
- 1/2 cup salt
- 2 ears corn

Direction
- Stir water, sugar, and salt together until the sugar and salt dissolves in a container large enough to hold the corn.
- Submerge corn in the brine; soak at least 1 hour.
- Preheat oven to 350 degrees F (175 degrees C).
- Remove corn from the brine, shake to remove excess liquid, and cook directly on an oven rack for 1 hour.

Nutrition Information

- Calories: 271 calories
- Total Fat: 1.1 g
- Cholesterol: 0 mg
- Sodium: 28 mg
- Total Carbohydrate: 67.1 g
- Protein: 2.9 g

Baked Potatoes on the Grill

"This is a recipe I use to throw a potato on the grill while I am grilling. I like how it makes the skin crispy and the center soft. Use whatever toppings you like, as in butter, sour cream, cheese, and bacon bits."

Serving: 2 | Prep: 5 m | Cook: 1 h | Ready in: 1 h 5 m

Ingredients
- 2 russet potatoes
- 1/4 teaspoon olive oil
- salt to taste
- 2 sheets aluminum foil

Direction
- Warm up the grill to medium heat.
- Wash and dry potatoes. Poke potatoes all over with a fork. Rub with olive oil and sprinkle with salt. Roll each potato up in aluminum foil and fold the ends in. Place potatoes on the grill and close the lid. Grill until fork-tender, rotating every 15 minutes or so, about 1 hour.

Nutrition Information
- Calories: 229 calories
- Total Fat: 0.8 g
- Cholesterol: 0 mg
- Sodium: 92 mg
- Total Carbohydrate: 51.2 g
- Protein: 6.1 g

Baked Tomato Slices

"A delicious way to top leftover pasta!"

Serving: 2 | Prep: 10 m | Cook: 5 m | Ready in: 15 m

Ingredients
- olive oil, divided, or as needed
- 1 large tomato, cut into 1/2-inch-thick slices
- 1 sprig fresh rosemary, leaves stripped and finely chopped
- 1 clove garlic, minced
- salt and ground black pepper to taste

Direction

- Preheat oven to 350 degrees F (175 degrees C). Brush baking sheet with about 1 tablespoon olive oil.
- Arrange tomato slices on the baking sheet. Sprinkle rosemary and garlic over tomatoes and brush with remaining olive oil; season with salt and pepper.
- Bake in the preheated oven until tomatoes are tender, 5 to 10 minutes.

Nutrition Information
- Calories: 138 calories
- Total Fat: 13.7 g
- Cholesterol: 0 mg
- Sodium: 5 mg
- Total Carbohydrate: 4.1 g
- Protein: 0.9 g

Balsamic Brown Sugar Carrots

"Yum."

Serving: 2 | Prep: 10 m | Cook: 15 m | Ready in: 25 m
Ingredients

- 1 tablespoon olive oil
- 2 carrots, cut into rounds, or more to taste
- 1 dash grill seasoning (such as Weber® Veggie Grill™ Seasoning)
- 2 tablespoons balsamic vinaigrette dressing (such as Newman's Own®)
- 1/2 teaspoon brown sugar

Direction
- Heat olive oil in a skillet over medium-low heat. Add carrots to the skillet and season with grill seasoning; cook and stir until lightly golden, 8 to 10 minutes. Carefully pour balsamic dressing over carrots; cook and stir until dressing is slightly reduced, about 3 minutes. Add brown sugar to carrots and cook until dissolved, about 2 minutes.

Nutrition Information
- Calories: 139 calories
- Total Fat: 11.4 g
- Cholesterol: 0 mg
- Sodium: 240 mg
- Total Carbohydrate: 9.6 g
- Protein: 0.7 g

BeerBoiled Corn on the Cob

"These quick snacks are one of a kind. Enjoy!"

Serving: 6 | Prep: 10 m | Cook: 20 m | Ready in: 30 m

Ingredients

- 3/4 cup beer
- 6 ears fresh corn, shucked
- 2 tablespoons butter
- 1/4 teaspoon salt
- 1/4 teaspoon seafood seasoning (such as Old Bay®)

Direction

- Bring beer to a boil in a large pot. Add corn, butter, salt, and seafood seasoning. Reduce heat to low; cover and cook, turning occasionally, until corn is tender, about 15 minutes.

Nutrition Information

- Calories: 125 calories
- Total Fat: 4.9 g
- Cholesterol: 10 mg
- Sodium: 162 mg
- Total Carbohydrate: 18.3 g
- Protein: 3.1 g

BlackEyed Peas Spicy Style

"A spicy twist on black-eyed peas."

Serving: 3 | Prep: 10 m | Cook: 30 m | Ready in: 40 m

Ingredients

- 1 (15.5 ounce) can black-eyed peas with liquid
- 1/2 onion, chopped
- minced jalapeno pepper to taste
- ground black pepper to taste

Direction

- In a medium-size pot, combine black-eyed peas, onion, jalapeno peppers, and black pepper (to taste). Heat all ingredients to simmer, let cook 30 minutes. Enjoy!

Nutrition Information

- Calories: 119 calories
- Total Fat: 0.8 g
- Cholesterol: 0 mg
- Sodium: 433 mg
- Total Carbohydrate: 21.4 g
- Protein: 7.1 g

Boiled Potatoes with Chives

"Simple but very good. Substitute new potatoes for the red if you prefer."

Serving: 4 | Prep: 15 m | Cook: 10 m | Ready in: 25 m

Ingredients

- 3 tablespoons unsalted butter, softened
- 2 pounds very small red potatoes, scrubbed
- salt and ground black pepper to taste
- 3 tablespoons finely chopped fresh chives

Direction

- Place butter in a serving bowl.
- Place potatoes into a large pot and cover with salted water by 1 inch; bring to a boil. Reduce heat to medium-low and simmer until tender, 10 to 15 minutes. Drain and cool until potatoes can be handled; cut potatoes in half.
- Place potatoes into serving bowl with butter, season with salt and black pepper, and toss with chives until potatoes are coated.

Nutrition Information

- Calories: 236 calories
- Total Fat: 9 g
- Cholesterol: 23 mg
- Sodium: 15 mg
- Total Carbohydrate: 36.2 g
- Protein: 4.5 g

Bok Choy Stir Fry

"This quick and easy recipe for bok choy stir fry goes nicely with any meat. I like to add 1/4 teaspoon chicken soup base (such as Penzey's®) to the hot bok choy. You can substitute 1/4 teaspoon ground ginger for the fresh ginger, if desired."

Serving: 2 | Prep: 5 m | Cook: 5 m | Ready in: 10 m

Ingredients
- 1 tablespoon olive oil
- 1 clove garlic, minced, or more to taste
- 1 teaspoon minced fresh ginger root
- 5 heads baby bok choy, ends trimmed and leaves separated
- 2 tablespoons water

Direction
- Heat olive oil in a large skillet over high heat. Cook and stir garlic and ginger in hot oil until fragrant, about 30 seconds. Stir bok choy into garlic mixture, add water, cover the skillet, and cook until bok choy wilts and is desired texture, about 2 minutes.

Nutrition Information
- Calories: 95 calories
- Total Fat: 7.3 g
- Cholesterol: 0 mg
- Sodium: 163 mg
- Total Carbohydrate: 6.1 g
- Protein: 3.9 g

Bourbon Glazed Carrots

"Sweet carrots are drizzled in a warm buttery sauce flavored with bourbon."

Serving: 8 | Prep: 10 m | Cook: 20 m | Ready in: 30 m

Ingredients

- 2 pounds carrots, peeled and sliced diagonally into 1/2-inch pieces
- 1/4 cup brown sugar
- 1/4 cup butter, melted
- 2 tablespoons bourbon, or more to taste

Direction

- Place carrots in a large pot and cover with water; bring to a boil. Reduce heat to medium-low and simmer until tender yet firm to the bite, 10 to 15 minutes. Drain and transfer to a serving bowl.
- Combine brown sugar, butter, and bourbon together in a saucepan; bring to a simmer. Cook and stir sauce until thickened, about 10 minutes. Pour sauce over carrots and serve immediately.

Nutrition Information

- Calories: 132 calories
- Total Fat: 6 g
- Cholesterol: 15 mg
- Sodium: 121 mg
- Total Carbohydrate: 17.6 g
- Protein: 1.1 g

Boursin Cheese Mashed Potatoes

"This is one of my favorite recipes. Really a crowd pleaser!"

Serving: 6 | Prep: 10 m | Cook: 15 m | Ready in: 25 m

Ingredients
- 4 pounds potatoes, peeled and cubed
- 1 quart buttermilk
- 1 (8 ounce) container garlic-and-herb spreadable cheese (such as Boursin®)

Direction
- Place potatoes into a large pot and cover with salted water; bring to a boil. Reduce heat to medium-low and simmer until tender, about 8 minutes. Drain and return potatoes to the pot.
- Pour buttermilk over the potatoes and mash until creamy. Stir cheese into the potatoes until melted completely and smooth.

Nutrition Information
- Calories: 450 calories
- Total Fat: 18.1 g
- Cholesterol: 51 mg
- Sodium: 416 mg
- Total Carbohydrate: 62 g
- Protein: 14 g

Braised Cabbage with Bacon

"Great side dish for about anything. Quick and easy, you can change or add seasonings if desired... but is straight-up good as-is."

Serving: 4 | Prep: 15 m | Cook: 12 m | Ready in: 27 m
Ingredients

- 1 teaspoon oil
- 1 onion, thinly sliced
- 1/2 (6 ounce) package Canadian-style bacon, chopped, or to taste
- 1 head white cabbage, thinly sliced
- 1 (12 fluid ounce) can or bottle beer

Direction

- Heat oil in a large stockpot over medium heat; cook and stir onion and bacon until fragrant, 2 to 4 minutes. Add cabbage and mix well; pour in beer. Cover stockpot and simmer, stirring occasionally, until cabbage is tender, 10 to 15 minutes.

Nutrition Information

- Calories: 178 calories
- Total Fat: 3 g
- Cholesterol: 11 mg
- Sodium: 358 mg
- Total Carbohydrate: 25.9 g
- Protein: 9.2 g

Brazilian Grilled Pineapple

"Favorite at a Brazilian steakhouse in Dallas. Not sure if this is the exact recipe they use but it tastes very close. Great side for kabobs and steak."

Serving: 6 | Prep: 10 m | Cook: 10 m | Ready in: 20 m

Ingredients
- 1 cup brown sugar
- 2 teaspoons ground cinnamon
- 1 pineapple - peeled, cored, and cut into 6 wedges

Direction

- Preheat an outdoor grill for medium-high heat and lightly oil the grate.
- Whisk brown sugar and cinnamon together in a bowl. Pour sugar mixture into a large resealable plastic bag. Place pineapple wedges in bag and shake to coat each wedge.
- Grill pineapple wedges on the preheated grill until heated through, 3 to 5 minutes per side.

Nutrition Information
- Calories: 255 calories
- Total Fat: 0.3 g
- Cholesterol: 0 mg
- Sodium: 13 mg
- Total Carbohydrate: 66.4 g
- Protein: 1.3 g

Breaded and Baked Zucchini

"Tangy breaded zucchini is baked until soft."

Serving: 2 | Prep: 15 m | Cook: 30 m | Ready in: 45 m
Ingredients

- 2 tablespoons brown mustard
- 2 tablespoons fat free Italian salad dressing
- 1/3 cup seasoned bread crumbs
- 1 zucchini, sliced 1/4-inch thick

Direction

- Preheat oven to 325 degrees F (165 degrees C).
- Mix mustard and Italian dressing together in a bowl. Place bread crumbs in a separate bowl. Dip zucchini slices in the mustard mixture; coat with bread crumbs. Arrange coated zucchini in a casserole dish.
- Bake in the preheated oven until soft, about 30 minutes.

Nutrition Information

- Calories: 111 calories
- Total Fat: 3.1 g
- Cholesterol: 1 mg
- Sodium: 757 mg
- Total Carbohydrate: 17.1 g
- Protein: 4.5 g

Broccoli and Cheese Nuggets

"It is not always easy to make children eat vegetables. Mine are teenagers now, but they still love this recipe of broccoli and cheese nuggets that I have been making for them since they were little. These delicious broccoli and cheese nuggets are not difficult to prepare and they take little time. This recipe is eaten very well as light lunch, as a side dish, and even as a snack. You can serve it as is, but accompanied with a dip it is even tastier. Here are some examples of dip that go very well with these broccoli and cheese nuggets: ranch dip, Asian dip, sour cream, and salsa."

Serving: 8 | Prep: 15 m | Cook: 25 m | Ready in: 40 m

Ingredients
- 4 cups finely chopped broccoli florets
- 2 cups shredded Cheddar cheese
- 2 eggs
- 1/2 cup dry bread crumbs

Direction

- Preheat oven to 375 degrees F (190 degrees C). Line a baking sheet with parchment paper.
- Mix broccoli, Cheddar cheese, eggs, and bread crumbs together in a large bowl. Roll into small balls with your hands. Flatten the balls into thick patties and place on the baking sheet.
- Bake in the preheated oven until tops are golden brown, about 15 minutes. Flip patties over and continue baking until opposite side is golden brown, about 10 minutes more.

Nutrition Information

- Calories: 173 calories

- Total Fat: 11.1 g
- Cholesterol: 76 mg
- Sodium: 257 mg
- Total Carbohydrate: 8.2 g
- Protein: 10.7 g

Broccoli Noodles and Cheese Casserole

"This is a quick and easy recipe if you are in a hurry -- just noodles, broccoli, cottage cheese and Cheddar. My daughter loves it. It's always a hit."

Serving: 8 | Cook: 30 m | Ready in: 30 m

Ingredients
- 1 (16 ounce) package egg noodles
- 1 head broccoli, cut into florets
- 2 cups cottage cheese
- 2 cups shredded Cheddar cheese

Direction
- Preheat oven to 350 degrees F (175 degrees C). Bring a large pot of lightly salted water to a boil. Add pasta and cook for 8 to 10 minutes or until al dente; drain.
- Steam broccoli until bright green and tender, 5 to 10 minutes. Combine broccoli, pasta and cottage cheese in 2 quart baking dish; mix well.
- Sprinkle pasta mixture with Cheddar cheese and bake for 8 to 10 minutes, until cheese is bubbly.

Nutrition Information
- Calories: 374 calories
- Total Fat: 14.8 g
- Cholesterol: 78 mg
- Sodium: 407 mg
- Total Carbohydrate: 39.5 g
- Protein: 21 g

Broccoli Puree

"I am always creating yummy vegetable sides that are easy enough for my older mother to eat and this broccoli puree turned out delicious and is easy to make. The cream is the secret ingredient."

Serving: 4 | Prep: 10 m | Cook: 25 m | Ready in: 35 m

Ingredients
- 2 small heads broccoli
- 2 tablespoons butter
- 1/2 cup heavy cream
- salt and freshly ground black pepper to taste
- 1 pinch ground nutmeg

Direction
- Separate broccoli crowns into florets. Peel stalks and cut into 1/2-inch pieces.
- Bring a large pot of lightly salted water to a boil. Cook broccoli until lightly softened, about 5 minutes. Drain, rinse under cold running water, and drain again.
- Melt butter in a pot, add broccoli, and cook for 2 minutes. Pour in cream and cook over low heat until broccoli is soft, about 10 minutes. Season with salt, pepper, and nutmeg. Puree broccoli with an immersion blender until smooth.

Nutrition Information

- Calories: 201 calories
- Total Fat: 17.4 g
- Cholesterol: 56 mg
- Sodium: 136 mg
- Total Carbohydrate: 9.9 g
- Protein: 4.5 g

Broiled Asparagus with Goat Cheese

"An easy and unbelievable yummy recipe for oven-broiled asparagus finished with crumbled goat cheese."

Serving: 4 | Prep: 5 m | Cook: 10 m | Ready in: 15 m

Ingredients
- 1 pound fresh asparagus, trimmed
- 2 tablespoons olive oil
- 1/2 teaspoon dried basil
- salt and freshly ground black pepper to taste
- 5 ounces crumbled goat cheese

Direction
- Set an oven rack about 6 inches from the heat source and preheat the oven's broiler.
- Combine asparagus, olive oil, basil, salt, and pepper on a sheet pan and mix well.
- Broil in the preheated oven until asparagus is cooked through and easily pierced with a knife, about 10 minutes. Remove from the oven and sprinkle with goat cheese.

Nutrition Information
- Calories: 212 calories
- Total Fat: 17.5 g
- Cholesterol: 28 mg
- Sodium: 224 mg
- Total Carbohydrate: 5.4 g
- Protein: 10.2 g

Brown Rice Pilaf with Onions and Corn

"Quick, easy, and tasty."

Serving: 2 | Prep: 10 m | Cook: 55 m | Ready in: 1 h 5 m

Ingredients
- 1 tablespoon olive oil
- 1/2 cup fresh corn kernels
- 1/2 cup chopped onion
- 1/2 cup brown rice
- 1 1/4 cups chicken broth

Direction
- Heat olive oil in a small saucepan over medium heat. Add corn and onion; cook and stir until lightly browned, 5 to 7 minutes. Add rice and stir to coat with oil. Add chicken broth and bring to a boil. Cover and reduce heat to low. Cook until rice is tender, about 45 minutes.

Nutrition Information
- Calories: 259 calories
- Total Fat: 8.4 g
- Cholesterol: 4 mg
- Sodium: 731 mg
- Total Carbohydrate: 40.7 g
- Protein: 4.8 g

Brussels Sprouts ala Angela

"My friend Angela gave me this holiday hit recipe! Everyone loved it and was asking for the recipe. Brussels sprouts have never been a favorite of mine until now. Beef stock can be used in place of chicken stock. Great side dish with our Easter ham. ENJOY!"

Serving: 6 | Prep: 15 m | Cook: 25 m | Ready in: 40 m

Ingredients
- 6 slices bacon, diced
- 1 onion, diced
- 1 tablespoon minced garlic
- 1 cup chicken stock
- 2 (16 ounce) packages Brussels sprouts, trimmed and halved lengthwise

Direction
- Place the bacon, onion, and garlic in a large, deep skillet and cook over medium-high heat until the onions caramelize, 10 to 12 minutes.
- Pour the chicken stock into the pan; add the Brussels sprouts. Bring the liquid to a boil while scraping the browned bits of food off of the bottom of the pan with a wooden spoon. Stir the mixture so the sprouts are coated in the liquid
- Place a cover on the skillet and cook until the sprouts are cooked through yet firm, about 15 minutes.

Nutrition Information
- Calories: 212 calories
- Total Fat: 13.2 g
- Cholesterol: 19 mg
- Sodium: 387 mg
- Total Carbohydrate: 17.9 g

- Protein: 9 g

Brussels Sprouts with Bacon and Balsamic

"Delicious glazed sprouts. Our family loves them with lots of bacon. While we do enjoy them prepared lighter, this is a great quick side dish for a special meal. Also perfect for holiday get-togethers."

Serving: 8 | Prep: 15 m | Cook: 15 m | Ready in: 30 m

Ingredients
- 2 pounds Brussels sprouts, trimmed and halved lengthwise
- 6 slices bacon, or more to taste, thinly sliced
- salt and ground black pepper to taste (optional)
- 2/3 cup reduced balsamic vinegar, divided

Direction
- Combine Brussels sprouts and bacon in a cast iron skillet; season with salt and pepper. Cook, stirring occasionally, until Brussels sprouts start to brown, 15 to 20 minutes. Drizzle 1/2 cup of balsamic vinegar on top.
- Transfer Brussels sprouts and bacon to a serving platter; drizzle remaining balsamic vinegar on top.

Nutrition Information
- Calories: 99 calories
- Total Fat: 3.3 g
- Cholesterol: 8 mg
- Sodium: 212 mg
- Total Carbohydrate: 13.4 g
- Protein: 6.5 g

ButteredBraised Cabbage

"This will make you like cabbage in a whole different way."

Serving: 6 | Prep: 5 m | Cook: 10 m | Ready in: 18 m

Ingredients
- 1/4 cup butter, divided
- 1 head green cabbage, shredded
- ground black pepper to taste

Direction
- Heat 3 tablespoons butter in a large pot over medium-low heat until mostly melted. Add cabbage. Place remaining 1 tablespoon butter on top of the cabbage. Cover and cook until cabbage is tender, about 10 minutes. Uncover and stir cabbage to coat evenly with butter. Remove from heat and let stand, covered, about 3 minutes. Season with black pepper.

Nutrition Information
- Calories: 117 calories
- Total Fat: 7.9 g
- Cholesterol: 20 mg
- Sodium: 90 mg
- Total Carbohydrate: 11.5 g
- Protein: 2.6 g

Butternut Squash Paleo Porridge

"This recipe was made with the paleo 'diet' in mind. It's gluten-free, dairy-free, and has no added sugar. I needed an alternative to other paleo breakfasts since I also cannot have eggs. This is the   result.
Those with fewer restrictions might enjoy stirring in a bit of maple syrup, adding brown sugar, or topping with granola for extra crunch."

Serving: 3 | Prep: 10 m | Cook: 50 m | Ready in: 1 h

Ingredients
- 1 butternut squash, halved and seeded
- water as needed
- 1/4 cup coconut milk, or to taste
- 1/2 teaspoon ground cinnamon
- 1 tablespoon chopped walnuts

Direction
- Preheat oven to 350 degrees F (175 degrees C).
- Place butternut squash halves, cut-side up, in a baking dish; fill dish with 1/4 inch of water.
- Bake in the preheated oven until softened, 50 to 60 minutes. Cool squash.
- Scoop squash flesh into a bowl and mash with a fork or potato masher until smooth. Stir coconut milk and cinnamon into squash; top with walnuts.

Nutrition Information
- Calories: 242 calories
- Total Fat: 6 g
- Cholesterol: 0 mg
- Sodium: 22 mg
- Total Carbohydrate: 49.9 g
- Protein: 4.9 g

ButterRoasted Cauliflower

"This is an unusual and tremendously tasty way to enjoy cauliflower. It's almost like discovering a new vegetable."

Serving: 4 | Prep: 10 m | Cook: 40 m | Ready in: 50 m

Ingredients

- 1 head cauliflower, cut into large florets
- 2 tablespoons butter, melted, or more to taste
- salt and ground black pepper to taste

Direction

- Preheat oven to 400 degrees F (200 degrees C). Line a baking sheet with a silicone baking mat.
- Spread cauliflower onto prepared baking sheet. Brush each piece of cauliflower with melted butter. Season with salt and black pepper.
- Roast in the preheated oven for 30 minutes. Flip cauliflower and continue roasting until tender and golden, about 10 minutes more.

Nutrition Information

- Calories: 87 calories
- Total Fat: 5.9 g
- Cholesterol: 15 mg
- Sodium: 123 mg
- Total Carbohydrate: 7.6 g
- Protein: 2.9 g

Buttery and Savory Acorn Squash

"A quick, simple side dish that is full of flavor. My daughter and I love this way of preparing squash."

Serving: 4 | Prep: 10 m | Cook: 7 m | Ready in: 17 m

Ingredients

- 2 small acorn squashes - peeled, seeded, and cut into 1-inch cubes
- 6 fresh sage leaves, shredded
- 1/2 cup butter, cut in small pieces
- salt and ground black pepper to taste

Direction

- Put squash in a microwave-safe bowl; add sage. Dot squash with butter pieces; season with salt and pepper. Cover bowl tightly with plastic wrap.
- Cook in microwave oven set on High for 5 minutes. Stir squash to coat in melted butter while checking cubes for softness. Replace plastic and continue to cook until completely tender, 2 to 4 minutes.

Nutrition Information

- Calories: 267 calories
- Total Fat: 23.2 g
- Cholesterol: 61 mg
- Sodium: 207 mg
- Total Carbohydrate: 16.4 g
- Protein: 1.5 g

Buttery Garlic Green Beans

"Only fresh green beans and garlic will do for this easy, healthy, and flavorful side dish."

Serving: 4 | Prep: 10 m | Cook: 10 m | Ready in: 20 m

Ingredients
- 1 pound fresh green beans, trimmed and snapped in half
- 3 tablespoons butter
- 3 cloves garlic, minced
- 2 pinches lemon pepper
- salt to taste

Direction
- Place green beans into a large skillet and cover with water; bring to a boil. Reduce heat to medium-low and simmer until beans start to soften, about 5 minutes. Drain water. Add butter to green beans; cook and stir until butter is melted, 2 to 3 minutes.
- Cook and stir garlic with green beans until garlic is tender and fragrant, 3 to 4 minutes. Season with lemon pepper and salt.

Nutrition Information
- Calories: 116 calories
- Total Fat: 8.8 g
- Cholesterol: 23 mg
- Sodium: 222 mg
- Total Carbohydrate: 8.9 g
- Protein: 2.3 g

Buttery Pecan Green Beans

"Sidney loved these."

Serving: 4 | Prep: 5 m | Cook: 10 m | Ready in: 15 m

Ingredients

- 1 (12 ounce) package frozen French-cut green beans (such as Kroger® Private Selection®, thawed
- 1 tablespoon butter
- 1/4 cup pecan pieces
- 1 pinch salt, or more to taste

Direction

- Place a steamer insert into a saucepan and fill with water to just below the bottom of the steamer. Bring water to a boil; add green beans, cover, and steam until tender, 2 to 6 minutes.
- Melt butter in a large skillet over medium heat. Cook pecans in melted butter until lightly browned; add green beans and stir to coat in butter. Season beans with salt.

Nutrition Information

- Calories: 98 calories
- Total Fat: 7.9 g
- Cholesterol: 8 mg
- Sodium: 24 mg
- Total Carbohydrate: 6.8 g
- Protein: 2 g

Cabbage Balushka or Cabbage and Noodles

"This Hungarian favorite is cabbage, onions, and egg noodles cooked in butter. Salt and pepper to taste. So easy, so good."

Serving: 6 | Prep: 15 m | Cook: 10 m | Ready in: 25 m

Ingredients
- 1 (16 ounce) package egg noodles
- 1/2 cup butter
- 1 large onion, chopped
- 1 head cabbage, cored and chopped
- salt and ground black pepper to taste

Direction
- Fill a large pot with lightly salted water and bring to a rolling boil. Stir in egg noodles and return to a boil. Cook noodles uncovered, stirring occasionally, until tender but still slightly firm, about 5 minutes. Drain well.
- Melt butter in a large skillet or wok over medium heat; cook and stir onion until browned, about 8 minutes.
- Cook and stir cabbage into onions until cabbage has wilted, another 5 to 8 minutes.
- Gently stir cooked noodles into cabbage mixture; season with salt and black pepper to taste.

Nutrition Information
- Calories: 482 calories
- Total Fat: 18.9 g
- Cholesterol: 103 mg
- Sodium: 161 mg
- Total Carbohydrate: 67 g
- Protein: 13.5 g

Cabbage Steaks

"One of my favorite side dishes, as it's very easy to make! I personally love garlic so I go crazy with it, but put as much as is good for you. This is a very simple recipe and you can put as much or as little of the seasonings you want."

Serving: 6 | Prep: 15 m | Cook: 45 m | Ready in: 1 h

Ingredients
- 1 head cabbage
- 2 tablespoons light olive oil
- 2 tablespoons minced garlic
- 1/2 teaspoon salt, or to taste
- 1/2 teaspoon ground black pepper, or to taste

Direction
- Preheat oven to 350 degrees F (175 degrees C).
- Cut the bottom off of the cabbage and set it so that the flat end is on the cutting board; cut into 1-inch thick slices. Arrange slices in a single layer in a large casserole dish.
- Drizzle olive oil over the cabbage slices and top with garlic. Season cabbage with salt and pepper. Cover the dish with aluminum foil.
- Bake in preheated oven until the cabbage core is easily pierced with a fork, about 45 minutes.

Nutrition Information
- Calories: 94 calories
- Total Fat: 4.7 g
- Cholesterol: 0 mg
- Sodium: 230 mg
- Total Carbohydrate: 12.4 g
- Protein: 2.7 g

Cacio e Pepe e Fagioli and Stuff

"I'm a little bit Italian, but I certainly can't say much in Italian. That's okay, because this recipe speaks for me. This was one of those, 'What can I do with what I have in the cupboard?' recipes, partially inspired by trying Cacio e Pepe ('Cheese and Pepper') earlier this year. It turned out great and I think you'll think so too! Serve with your favorite Italian main dish and enjoy!"

Serving: 4 | Prep: 10 m | Cook: 20 m | Ready in: 30 m

Ingredients

- 1 (15 ounce) can sweet peas, partially drained
- 1 (15 ounce) can cannellini beans, undrained
- 2 tablespoons butter
- 3/4 cup grated Parmesan cheese
- 2 teaspoons freshly ground black pepper, or more to taste

Direction

- Empty sweet peas and cannellini beans into a saucepan; cook and stir over medium-high heat until heated through and 1/3 of the liquid has evaporated, about 10 minutes. Stir butter into pea mixture until melted, 2 to 3 minutes. Reduce heat to medium.
- Stir Parmesan cheese and black pepper into pea mixture. Cook, stirring occasionally, until creamy and thickened, 5 to 10 minutes.

Nutrition Information

- Calories: 251 calories
- Total Fat: 10.5 g
- Cholesterol: 28 mg
- Sodium: 824 mg
- Total Carbohydrate: 25.3 g
- Protein: 13.4 g

Campfire Potatoes and Carrots

"This is a fast, easy, and delicious way to make potatoes on the campfire. I make them in the oven as well because they are so great."

Serving: 4 | Prep: 15 m | Cook: 45 m | Ready in: 1 h

Ingredients
- 3 large potatoes, cut into cubes
- 2 carrots, cut into cubes
- 1 tablespoon butter
- 1 (1 ounce) package dry onion soup mix (such as Lipton®)

Direction
- Place a grill grate over your campfire.
- Lay a thick piece of aluminum foil onto a flat work surface. Pile potatoes and carrots into the middle of the foil. Put butter on the vegetables and sprinkle onion soup mix over the top.
- Fold opposite ends of the foil so they meet; roll together to form a seam. Roll remaining ends together to seal contents into a packet.
- Cook packet on the grill until the potatoes and carrots are completely tender, about 45 minutes.

Nutrition Information
- Calories: 272 calories
- Total Fat: 3.3 g
- Cholesterol: 8 mg
- Sodium: 680 mg
- Total Carbohydrate: 56.2 g
- Protein: 6.4 g

Carrots and Cranberries

"A very quick way to make fresh carrots into a tasty side dish. Even kids will like this."

Serving: 6 | Prep: 10 m | Cook: 12 m | Ready in: 27 m

Ingredients

- 2 (8 ounce) packages carrots, peeled and cut into chunks
- 1 cup dried cranberries, or more to taste
- 1/4 cup chicken broth
- 1/4 cup butter, melted
- 1/4 cup dark brown sugar
- 1 pinch ground cinnamon, or to taste

Direction

- Put carrots and cranberries into a microwave-safe dish. Mix chicken broth, butter, and brown sugar together in a bowl; drizzle over the carrot mixture and stir to coat.
- Cook in microwave on High for 4 minutes.
- Continue cooking in microwave until carrots are tender, about 8 minutes more; cool at room temperature for 5 minutes and sprinkle with cinnamon.

Nutrition Information

- Calories: 195 calories
- Total Fat: 7.9 g
- Cholesterol: 21 mg
- Sodium: 149 mg
- Total Carbohydrate: 32.9 g
- Protein: 0.8 g

Cauliflower Puree

"This simple but surprisingly flavorful puree is a satisfying stand-in for mashed potatoes, and it couldn't be easier. There's no cream in it and only a teensy touch of butter, so it's good for anyone counting calories or carbs. It pleases the meat-and-potatoes eaters at my table, even though it contains neither."

Serving: 4 | Prep: 10 m | Cook: 10 m | Ready in: 20 m

Ingredients
- salt to taste
- 1 head cauliflower, cut into florets
- 1 tablespoon butter

Direction
- Bring a 4-quart pot of salted water to a boil; add cauliflower and simmer until tender, 7 to 10 minutes. Drain cauliflower, reserving 1 cup cooking liquid.
- Blend cauliflower and 1/4 cup cooking liquid in a blender until smooth, adding more water until desired consistency is reached. Add butter and pulse until incorporated; season with salt.

Nutrition Information
- Calories: 61 calories
- Total Fat: 3 g
- Cholesterol: 8 mg
- Sodium: 102 mg
- Total Carbohydrate: 7.6 g
- Protein: 2.9 g

Cauliflower Radish Garlic Mash

"A healthier low-carb alternative for mashed potatoes with the kick of radish!"

Serving: 8 | Prep: 20 m | Cook: 10 m | Ready in: 30 m

Ingredients
- 4 cloves garlic, roughly chopped, or more to taste
- 2 heads cauliflower, roughly chopped
- 2 cups roughly chopped radishes
- freshly ground black pepper to taste
- 1 pinch salt to taste (optional)

Direction
- Combine water and garlic in a large pot; bring to a boil. Add cauliflower and radishes; cook and stir until cauliflower is tender and easily pierced with a fork, 5 to 10 minutes. Strain, reserving cooking liquid; place the cauliflower mixture in a bowl.
- Blend the cauliflower mixture with a handheld mixer, thinning with some cooking liquid, until smooth. Season with pepper and salt.

Nutrition Information
- Calories: 40 calories
- Total Fat: 0.2 g
- Cholesterol: 0 mg
- Sodium: 66 mg
- Total Carbohydrate: 8.4 g
- Protein: 3 g

Cheesy Asparagus Casserole

"This is a great recipe for fresh asparagus. Very simple and kids as well as adults love it. The buttered bread on top gives it just enough crunch, and the cheese it what makes the kids ask for seconds."

Serving: 12 | Prep: 10 m | Cook: 28 m | Ready in: 38 m

Ingredients
- 15 spears fresh asparagus, cut into 1-inch pieces, or more to taste
- 1 tablespoon butter, softened, or as needed
- 3 slices bread, divided
- 1 (10.75 ounce) can condensed cream of mushroom soup
- 4 ounces processed cheese food (such as Velveeta®), cubed

Direction
- Bring 1/2 inch water to a boil in a saucepan. Add asparagus, cover, and steam until tender, about 8 minutes. Drain.
- Spread a thin layer of butter onto each bread slice. Cut bread into cubes.
- Stir cream of mushroom soup, processed cheese food, and 2/3 of buttered bread cubes together in a bowl; stir in asparagus. Transfer asparagus mixture to a 9x13-inch baking dish; top with remaining bread cubes.
- Bake in the preheated oven until bread is golden brown, about 20 minutes.

Nutrition Information
- Calories: 82 calories
- Total Fat: 5 g
- Cholesterol: 10 mg
- Sodium: 332 mg
- Total Carbohydrate: 6.4 g
- Protein: 3.1 g

Cheesy Kale Chips

"An addictive alternative made with nutritional yeast. Who would have thought that leafy green chips loaded with nutrients could be so addictive? Nutritional yeast is deactivated yeast; it's not alive and has a slightly cheesy flavor which many vegans like to use as a cheese substitute. It can be found at most health food stores and some big-chain grocery stores."

Serving: 6 | Prep: 5 m | Cook: 45 m | Ready in: 50 m

Ingredients
- 2 tablespoons extra virgin olive oil
- 1 bunch curly kale, torn
- 1/2 cup nutritional yeast
- 1/3 teaspoon salt

Direction
- Preheat oven to 200 degrees F (95 degrees C).
- Drizzle olive oil over the kale in a large bowl and sprinkle with the nutritional yeast and salt. Stir with your hands to coat kale.
- Spread kale onto baking sheets.
- Bake in preheated oven until kale begins to get slightly crisp; rotate racks and flip the chips, and continue baking until completely crisp, 45 to 60 minutes total. Make sure to keep an eye on them to make sure they don't burn; if you notice certain chips ready much sooner than others, take them out.

Nutrition Information
- Calories: 111 calories
- Total Fat: 5.5 g
- Cholesterol: 0 mg
- Sodium: 165 mg
- Total Carbohydrate: 10.8 g
- Protein: 7.8 g

Chef Johns FiveSpice Carrots

"These five-spice roast carrots are amazingly aromatic and delicious. The ingredients are so simple. Exotic, but familiar and not too exotic."

Serving: 6 | Prep: 15 m | Cook: 30 m | Ready in: 45 m

Ingredients
- 7 large carrots, peeled and cut in half lengthwise
- 2 tablespoons vegetable oil
- 1/2 teaspoon Chinese five-spice powder
- salt to taste

Direction
- Preheat oven to 375 degrees F (190 degrees C).
- Cut halved carrots in half again crosswise on the diagonal. Place carrots into a 2-quart baking dish and drizzle with vegetable oil; sprinkle with 5-spice powder and salt to taste. Toss lightly to coat carrots with oil and seasoning. Arrange carrots into an even layer.
- Roast carrots in the preheated oven for 15 minutes; check for tenderness and stir if desired. Continue roasting until tender, 15 to 20 more minutes.

Nutrition Information
- Calories: 75 calories
- Total Fat: 4.8 g
- Cholesterol: 0 mg
- Sodium: 58 mg
- Total Carbohydrate: 8.2 g
- Protein: 0.8 g

Chic Green Beans

"Easy green beans that complement many dishes!"

Serving: 3 | Prep: 10 m | Cook: 10 m | Ready in: 20 m

Ingredients

- 1/2 pound fresh green beans, trimmed
- 2 tablespoons butter
- 1/2 cup sliced mushrooms
- 1/4 cup sliced almonds
- 1 pinch garlic salt, or to taste
- ground black pepper to taste

Direction

- Bring a pot water to a boil; add green beans and cook until just tender, 6 to 8 minutes. Drain.
- Meanwhile, melt butter in a skillet over medium heat. Cook and stir mushrooms and almonds until tender, about 3 minutes; stir in green beans. Season with garlic salt and black pepper.

Nutrition Information

- Calories: 142 calories
- Total Fat: 11.8 g
- Cholesterol: 20 mg
- Sodium: 170 mg
- Total Carbohydrate: 7.7 g
- Protein: 3.7 g

Cinnamon Apples

"I created this recipe last fall, and my family loved it! It is a nice warm side dish for those chilly autumn nights."

Serving: 4 | Prep: 5 m | Cook: 2 m | Ready in: 7 m

Ingredients

- 2 apples, diced
- 1 teaspoon white sugar
- 1/2 teaspoon ground cinnamon

Direction
- Place apples in a microwave-safe bowl; heat in microwave for 30 seconds. Sprinkle sugar and cinnamon over apples and stir to coat. Heat apples in microwave until soft and warm, about 1 minute more.

Nutrition Information
- Calories: 41 calories
- Total Fat: 0.1 g
- Cholesterol: 0 mg
- Sodium: < 1 mg
- Total Carbohydrate: 10.8 g
- Protein: 0.2 g

CitrusBacon Green Beans

"Green beans are bland. Mix it up with citrus juices and bacon bits for a new taste! Seasonings can be added as desired for taste!"

Serving: 4 | Prep: 5 m | Cook: 10 m | Ready in: 15 m

Ingredients
- 2 tablespoons butter
- 1 (14.5 ounce) can French style green beans, drained
- 1 tablespoon lemon juice
- 1 tablespoon lime juice
- 3 ounces bacon bits

Direction
- Melt butter in a skillet over medium heat. Stir green beans into melted butter. Add lemon juice and lime juice; simmer for 3 minutes.
- Stir bacon bits into green beans and simmer until beans are heated through and flavors blend, about 5 minutes.

Nutrition Information
- Calories: 146 calories
- Total Fat: 10.3 g
- Cholesterol: 30 mg
- Sodium: 1045 mg
- Total Carbohydrate: 4.1 g
- Protein: 10.1 g

Clean Eating Refried Beans

"This is a healthy alternative for the typical saturated fatty refried beans. Don't let the time scare you off. I soak them while I sleep and cook them during the day, so by dinner it is only 10 minutes from stove top to table. Not much longer than preparing a processed can product."

Serving: 18 | Prep: 10 m | Cook: 8 h 5 m | Ready in: 16 h 15 m

Ingredients
- 3 cups dried pinto beans
- 16 1/2 cups water, divided
- 3 tablespoons olive oil
- 1/2 teaspoon salt
- 1/4 teaspoon ground black pepper

Direction
- Place beans in a slow cooker and cover with 8 cups water; soak for 8 to 10 hours.
- Drain and rinse beans and return to slow cooker; top with 8 cups fresh water.
- Cook beans on Low for 8 to 10 hours. Drain.
- Combine 1/2 cup water, beans, olive oil, salt, and pepper in a skillet over medium heat; mash beans to desired consistency.

Nutrition Information
- Calories: 132 calories
- Total Fat: 2.6 g
- Cholesterol: 0 mg
- Sodium: 75 mg
- Total Carbohydrate: 20.1 g
- Protein: 6.9 g

Coconut Jasmine Rice

"This is one of my favorite rice recipes. It goes great with just about anything! Try a ginger chicken main dish with it!"

Serving: 6 | Prep: 10 m | Cook: 20 m | Ready in: 30 m

Ingredients
- 1 (14 ounce) can coconut milk
- 1 1/4 cups water
- 1 teaspoon white sugar
- 1 pinch salt
- 1 1/2 cups jasmine rice

Direction
- Stir coconut milk, water, sugar, and salt together in a saucepan over medium heat until sugar dissolves. Add rice; bring to a boil, cover the saucepan, reduce heat to low, and simmer until rice is tender and liquid is absorbed, 18 to 20 minutes.

Nutrition Information
- Calories: 302 calories
- Total Fat: 13.9 g
- Cholesterol: 0 mg
- Sodium: 10 mg
- Total Carbohydrate: 40.9 g
- Protein: 4.5 g

Coconut Quinoa

"A nice change from plain old grains. Quinoa has become a staple in our home because it only takes about 15 minutes to cook as opposed to 45 minutes for brown rice. I use canned coconut milk or coconut milk from the carton interchangeably. However, the coconut milk from the carton is sweetened, which my family likes but might not be right with some main dishes."

Serving: 6 | Prep: 10 m | Cook: 10 m | Ready in: 20 m

Ingredients

- 1 cup quinoa
- 2 cups coconut milk
- 2 tablespoons flaked coconut (optional)
- salt to taste

Direction
- Bring quinoa, coconut milk, and flaked coconut to a boil in a saucepan. Reduce heat to medium-low and simmer, stirring occasionally, until the quinoa is tender and the water has been absorbed, 10 to 15 minutes; season with salt.

Nutrition Information
- Calories: 266 calories
- Total Fat: 19 g
- Cholesterol: 0 mg
- Sodium: 12 mg
- Total Carbohydrate: 20.8 g
- Protein: 5.7 g

Corn and Bacon

"A very simple, quick side dish of corn and diced bacon. The salty zing of the bacon with the freshness of the corn is very delicious. This is a favorite of mine to prepare due to the ease of cooking and the low-carb nature of the dish."

Serving: 5 | Prep: 5 m | Cook: 10 m | Ready in: 15 m
Ingredients

- 6 slices bacon, diced
- 2 cups fresh corn kernels
- 1 pinch salt and ground black pepper to taste

Direction

- Spread bacon into a large skillet and place over medium-high heat; cook and stir until bacon is crisp, 7 to 10 minutes. Remove bacon with a slotted spoon to a plate lined with paper towel.
- Stir corn into the bacon grease in the skillet to coat; sauté until hot, 3 to 5 minutes. Stir bacon with the corn; season with salt and pepper

Nutrition Information

- Calories: 207 calories
- Total Fat: 15.9 g
- Cholesterol: 23 mg
- Sodium: 320 mg
- Total Carbohydrate: 11.9 g
- Protein: 5.9 g

Corn and Jalapenos

"Great combination of corn and peppers!"

Serving: 3 | Prep: 10 m | Cook: 15 m | Ready in: 25 m

Ingredients

- 2 teaspoons olive oil
- 1 large jalapeno pepper, minced
- 2 tablespoons diced onion
- 1 1/2 cups frozen corn, thawed
- salt and ground black pepper to taste
- 1 tablespoon chopped fresh cilantro

Direction

- Heat olive oil over medium low heat. Cook and stir jalapeno pepper in hot oil until softened, about 5 minutes. Add onion; cook and stir until the onion is soft, about 2 minutes more. Add corn. Season mixture with salt and black pepper. Continue cooking and stirring until the corn is hot, about 5 minutes. Sprinkle cilantro over the mixture, stir, and simmer another 30 to 60 seconds.

Nutrition Information

- Calories: 104 calories
- Total Fat: 3.8 g
- Cholesterol: 0 mg
- Sodium: 3 mg
- Total Carbohydrate: 18 g
- Protein: 2.6 g

Corn On The Cob Easy Cleaning and Shucking

"No need to remove silk from corn on the cob. Fast and easy microwave recipe that is shucked without removing shucks or silk. If cooking more than one ear, simply increase cooking time by about two minutes."

Serving: 1 | Prep: 10 m | Cook: 5 m | Ready in: 15 m

Ingredients
- 1 ear corn on the cob, unhusked
- 1 teaspoon butter, or to taste
- salt to taste

Direction
- Place ear of corn in a microwave oven and cook on high for 2 minutes; flip corn over and cook on high until kernels are hot and steaming, another 2 minutes.
- Place corn ear on a cutting board, using a pot holder or folded kitchen towel, and cut off the bottom of the ear, exposing 1/4 to 1/2 inch of kernels. Hold the ear from the top and squeeze ear of corn out of the husk from top to bottom. Husks and silk will be left behind.
- Spread ear with butter and season with salt.

Nutrition Information
- Calories: 113 calories
- Total Fat: 5.1 g
- Cholesterol: 11 mg
- Sodium: 42 mg
- Total Carbohydrate: 17.1 g
- Protein: 2.9 g

Cottage Cheese Bake

"Yummy high-protein and low-fat recipe. You can use low-fat or fat-free cottage cheese."

Serving: 6 | Prep: 10 m | Cook: 20 m | Ready in: 30 m

Ingredients
- 2 cups low-fat cottage cheese
- 1 (10 ounce) package frozen chopped spinach, thawed and drained
- 2 eggs, beaten
- 1/2 cup grated Parmesan cheese
- 1 pinch garlic powder, or to taste (optional)
- 1 pinch salt and ground black pepper to taste

Direction
- Preheat oven to 350 degrees F (175 degrees C).
- Mix cottage cheese, spinach, eggs, and Parmesan cheese together in a bowl; pour into an 8-inch square baking dish and smooth into an even layer.
- Bake in preheated oven until the cheese is bubbling along the edges, 20 to 30 minutes. Season with garlic powder, salt, and pepper.

Nutrition Information
- Calories: 135 calories
- Total Fat: 5.3 g
- Cholesterol: 74 mg
- Sodium: 466 mg
- Total Carbohydrate: 5.2 g
- Protein: 16.8 g

Couscous Caprese

"A roasted tomato stuffed with couscous, fresh mozzarella, and basil makes a wonderful side dish. It's very pleasing to the eye and the mouth."

Serving: 4 | Prep: 10 m | Cook: 20 m | Ready in: 35 m

Ingredients
- 1 cup boiling water
- 1 cup couscous
- 4 tomatoes
- 16 leaves fresh basil
- 8 ounces fresh mozzarella cheese, diced
- 1/4 cup balsamic vinegar, or to taste

Direction
- Preheat oven to 350 degrees F (175 degrees C). Lightly grease a baking dish.
- Pour boiling water over couscous in a bowl. Cover bowl with plastic wrap. Let couscous soak until the water is completely absorbed, about 5 minutes.
- Slice the tops from tomatoes and take a very small slice of the bottoms so they will be stable upright. Use a spoon to remove and discard the tomato innards. Put tomatoes in the prepared baking dish.
- Bake tomatoes in the preheated oven until lightly charred at the edges, about 20 minutes.
- Line the inner walls of each tomato with 4 basil leaves.
- Toss mozzarella cheese with the couscous; stuff into tomatoes. Drizzle balsamic vinegar over the top of the stuffed tomatoes.

Nutrition Information
- Calories: 292 calories
- Total Fat: 9.4 g

- Cholesterol: 36 mg
- Sodium: 367 mg
- Total Carbohydrate: 32.6 g
- Protein: 18.8 g

Crack Potatoes

"They call these 'crack potatoes' because you can't stop eating them!"

Serving: 14 | Prep: 10 m | Cook: 45 m | Ready in: 55 m

Ingredients
- 1 (28 ounce) package frozen hash browns
- 2 (16 ounce) containers sour cream
- 2 cups shredded Cheddar cheese
- 1 (2 ounce) package real bacon bits
- 2 (1 ounce) packages ranch dressing mix

Direction
- Preheat oven to 400 degrees F (200 degrees C).
- Combine hash browns, sour cream, Cheddar cheese, bacon bits, and ranch dressing mix in a bowl; stir until mixed. Pour into a 9x12-inch baking pan.
- Bake in the preheated oven until potatoes are golden brown and cooked through, 45 to 60 minutes.

Nutrition Information
- Calories: 274 calories
- Total Fat: 23.3 g
- Cholesterol: 48 mg
- Sodium: 560 mg
- Total Carbohydrate: 15 g
- Protein: 8.9 g

Creamy Celery Root Mash

"This is a delicious and quick way to prepare a root veggie that isn't often talked about. Celeriac has a slightly tangy taste that is reminiscent of celery, but much subtler and has a fabulous flavor. Delicious!"

Serving: 6 | Prep: 10 m | Cook: 20 m | Ready in: 30 m

Ingredients
- 2 pounds celeriac (celery root), peeled and cut into 1/2-inch cubes
- 1/4 cup sour cream, or more to taste
- 1/2 teaspoon dried dill weed, or more to taste
- salt and ground black pepper to taste

Direction
- Place celeriac into a large pot and cover with salted water; bring to a boil. Reduce heat to medium-low and simmer until tender, about 20 minutes. Drain and transfer to a large bowl.
- Mash celeriac, sour cream, and dill together in a large bowl with a potato masher until smooth. Season with salt and pepper.

Nutrition Information
- Calories: 84 calories
- Total Fat: 2.5 g
- Cholesterol: 4 mg
- Sodium: 157 mg
- Total Carbohydrate: 14.4 g
- Protein: 2.6 g

Creamy Parmesan Polenta

"Easy and delicious creamy polenta. Makes a great side, appetizer, or base for a hearty stew."

Serving: 4 | Prep: 10 m | Cook: 5 m | Ready in: 15 m

Ingredients
- 1 (18 ounce) package polenta, cut into 1/2-inch cubes
- 1 cup chicken broth
- 1/2 cup grated Parmesan cheese
- 1 teaspoon ground black pepper
- 1 dash paprika

Direction
- Stir polenta and chicken broth together in a saucepan over medium heat; cook and stir until the polenta is heated through completely, about 5 minutes.
- Remove pan from heat. Stir Parmesan cheese, black pepper, and paprika with the polenta mixture.

Nutrition Information
- Calories: 533 calories
- Total Fat: 12.3 g
- Cholesterol: 18 mg
- Sodium: 1186 mg
- Total Carbohydrate: 87.1 g
- Protein: 18.9 g

Part 2

Marshmallow Fruit Dip

Marshmallows make a great treat while you are camping with the family. You can make so many variations with them. Marshmallow fruit dip is a great choice when it comes to satisfying your taste buds in a healthy manner.

Ingredients:

8 oz of Cream Cheese, softened at room temperature

6 oz of Cherry Yogurt

8 oz of Frozen Whipped Topping

7 oz of Marshmallow Cream

Seasonal fruits, any of your choice

Directions:

Thaw the frozen whipped topping by keeping it overnight in the refrigerator.

Take an electric mixer and mix together the cherry yogurt and the cream cheese until well blended. Fold in the whipped topping with the help of a spatula. In the end, fold in the marshmallow cream.

Serving Suggestions:

For serving, take out the dip in individual cups. You can also decorate the individual cups with any fruits of your choice while serving.

Mozzarella Sticks

Snack times have to be fun. Enjoy these tasty mozzarella sticks while watching your favorite game.

Ingredients:

1 package of mozzarella cheese sticks

2/3 cup of all-purpose flour

1 ½ cups of Italian style dried bread crumbs

1/3 cup of corn starch

2 slightly beaten eggs

Directions:

Beat the eggs in a bowl. In another bowl mix the corn starch and the flour until they are well combined.

If you require, you can add a little bit of salt into the breadcrumbs as well.

Heat enough oil in a wok and coat each mozzarella stick first into the flour, then eggs and in the end the bread crumbs. Deep fry until the sticks turn golden brown. Drain on a paper towel and serve with your favorite sauce.

Mushroom and Onion Tacos

Who says that you can't make tacos with limited ingredients. These mushroom and onion tacos are not only tasty but can make a great meal as well.

Ingredients:

¾ cup of red onion, thinly sliced

¾ cup of fresh Portobello mushrooms, stems removed

2 tablespoons of Taco seasoning, any of your choice

8 flour tortillas

Directions:

Clean the mushrooms and remove their stems. Slice the mushrooms and cut each slice into a half.

Take a non-stick pan and heat some oil in it. Add in the onion and cook them until they turn a nice golden brown.

Add in the mushrooms and cook until they become tender. Turn down the heat to low and in the seasoning. Mix the ingredients and cook for almost a minute. Add a few tablespoons of water in the mixture and bring it to a boil. Let the mixture cook until the water is absorbed.

Spoon out the filling into the tortillas and fold them up. Serve hot.

Nacho Potato Skins

Ingredients:

4-5 large potatoes, sliced as wedges

One cup of salsa (any variety)

Two cups of cheese sauce or soup

One teaspoon of vegetable oil

Directions:
Preheat oven to 400 degrees. In a large bowl, mix oil and potatoes until evenly covered.
Place potatoes on baking sheet and let cook for 20-25 minutes or until edges are crisp.
Using a medium saucepan, heat sauce until bubbly and mix in salsa.
Remove from heat and let cool before pouring on top of potato skins. Garnish with guacamole or sour cream.

Okra Gumbo

Okras are everybody's favorite, and if you really want to delight your taste buds, then you should definitely try out this okra gumbo recipe.

Ingredients:

2 packages of fresh okra,

2 cups of chopped celery

¾ cup of sweet onions

2 cans of stewed tomatoes

2 cloves of garlic, minced

Directions:

Heat some oil in a frying pan and add in the minced garlic and sweet onions. Cook until the onions become soft and translucent.

Add in the okra and cook for almost a minute. Now, stir in the stewed tomatoes along with the liquid and cook them for a few more minutes. At this point, you can add in the seasoning as well.

After 5 minutes or so, turn down the heat to low and let the stew simmer for at least half an hour.

Once the okra is well cooked, the tomatoes are dissolved into the okra and the liquid has dried up, you can serve the okra.

Peanut Butter Bars

If you have got a fussy eater at your place, then these tasty, easy-to-make peanut butter bars are going to solve your problem. Make them in batches and store them in an air tight jar for a few days.

Ingredients:

3 cups of quick cooking oats

1 cup of natural peanut butter

1 cup of brown sugar

Directions:

Grease a 9x9 inches pan or dish.

Take a medium sized non-stick saucepan and cook together the peanut butter and brown sugar until both the ingredients are well dissolved into each other. The mixture should have a liquid like consistency when it is ready.

At this moment, add in the oats. Let the oats cook on a medium low flame. Make sure to keep on stirring frequently, so that all the ingredients are combined.

Pour the mixture over the greased pan and let it set overnight in a refrigerator.

Serving Suggestions:

You can also use honey in place of the brown sugar and old fashioned oats instead of the quick cooking ones as well.

Pepper Rice Casserole

Ingredients:

Two cups of instant rice

One small can of chipotle peppers, in sauce

One small can of green chile or jalapeno peppers, drained

One can of cheddar cheese or creamed mushroom soup

One cup of cheese, (cheddar or jack, shredded)

Directions:

Preheat oven at 350 degrees and add ingredients except for cheese to large mixing bowl.

Add salt and ground black pepper to mixture, if desired.

Place inside casserole dish or Dutch oven and cover. Cook for 25-30 minutes and top with cheese.

Cook for 5-10 minutes, or until bubbly.

Pesto Pasta

Pesto pasta takes no time t take and does not require any fancy ingredients. Sprinkle some Parmesan on the top and eat hot.

Ingredients:

16 oz of pasta

2 ½ tablespoons of pesto

2 tablespoons of Parmesan cheese, grated

2 tablespoons of olive oil

Salt and pepper, according to taste

Directions:

Boil the pasta according to the package Directions. Drain with the help of a colander.

Take a medium sized pan and start making the pesto mixture by heating the olive oil in it. Add in the pesto, and salt and pepper. Cook for 5 minutes.

Mix the pasta into the pesto paste and take it out in a serving dish.

Pineapple Cranberry Salad

Ingredients:

One can (8 oz. Or more) of crushed pineapple

One can of whole cranberries, in juice

One small carton of yogurt, plain or vanilla

½ cup of walnuts

Directions:

Mix all ingredients in a medium bowl until even. Cover and chill for at least an hour before serving.

Potato Soup

Giving your family a nice homemade potato soup can make them fresh and fill their tummies on a long working day. Easy to make, this potato soup requires minimum amount of ingredients and does not require a long cooking time as well.

Ingredients:

6 cups of potatoes, boiled, cooled and mashed

½ cup of onion, finely chopped

2 cups of vegetable stock

½ cup of milk

1 tablespoon of butter, at room temperature

Directions:

Take a medium sized pot and melt the butter in it. Add in the onions, and sauté them until they turn a nice golden brown.

Add in the mashed potatoes and stir them. Cook for a few minutes and start adding the vegetable broth slowly and gradually. Bring the stock to a boil.

Start adding the milk slowly while continuously stirring the soup. The amount of milk you want to add entirely depends upon the consistency of the soup which you require.

In the end, season with salt and pepper and let the soup simmer on a low flame until it is properly heated.

Serving Suggestions:

Serve hot with French bread.

Pumpkin Pie Bars

Ingredients:

One (32 oz.) can of pumpkin (plain)

One box of yellow cake mix

Two teaspoons of agave nectar

One tablespoon of apple pie spice or cinnamon
Directions:
Preheat oven at 400 degrees. In a large mixing bowl, combine all ingredients and mix until smooth.
Pour inside baking pan and bake for 35-40 minutes.
Let cool for 10 minutes before slicing into square shapes.

Quick Chili

Ingredients:

One large can of kidney or black beans

One (8 oz.) can of tomato sauce

One cup of onion, chopped

Two teaspoons of all-purpose or chili seasoning

One can of jalapenos, chopped (optional)

Directions:
In a large pan, heat beans and other ingredients on medium heat and mix until bubbly.
Cover and let sit for about 10 minutes before serving.

Quick Fried Okra

Ingredients:

One box of cornbread mix

One pound of okra, either chopped to a ½ inch or whole

Salt and pepper to taste

One cup of vegetable oil

Directions:

Heat the oil on medium in large pan. Prepare mix as directed and add seasonings. Dip each piece inside batter. Shake off excess batter.

Carefully place okra inside oil and let brown on each side.

Drain on paper towel for at least five minutes before serving.

Quick Lasagna

Ingredients:

One box of pre-cooked lasagna noodles

3 cups (or 32 oz.) of marinara sauce

One cup of spinach, fresh or frozen

Two tablespoons of Italian Blend seasoning

Two cups of mozzarella cheese, shredded or crumbled
Directions:
Preheat oven at 350 degrees. Using a casserole dish or Dutch oven, place noodles flat and top with spinach, followed by enough pasta to cover.
Top with sauce and cook covered for about 20 minutes.
Uncover and add cheese; cook for an additional 10 minutes

Quick Mac-N-Cheese

Ingredients:

1 ½ cups of macaroni or small, dense pasta

One can of cheddar cheese soup

Two cups of bread crumbs (any variety)

One tablespoon of butter or margarine, melted

All-purpose seasoning or salt and pepper to taste
Directions:
Preheat oven to 375 degrees. Cook pasta as directed on package and drain before placing inside casserole dish or Dutch oven.
Pour soup on top of pasta, followed by seasoning. Let pasta cook for 15 minutes or until bubbly.
In a medium bowl, mix butter and bread crumbs and spread generous amount across pasta.
Cook for an additional 10 minutes.

Spicy Cactus Tacos

Ingredients:

2 cups of peeled cactus or nopales, chopped small

½ cup of carrots, shredded or chopped small

One large onion, chopped small

One small can of chipotle peppers

Salt and pepper to taste

One dozen corn tortillas

Directions:

In a medium saucepan, add carrots and onions with a ½ cup of water.

Cover and let cook for five minutes.

Add cactus, followed by seasonings.

Cover and let simmer for about 10 minutes.

Serve with tortillas

Spicy Corn Bake

Ingredients:

One box of cornbread mix

One small carton of sour cream or plain yogurt

One small can of jalapeno peppers

One small can of creamed corn

Two tablespoons of vegetable oil

Directions:

Preheat oven at 350 degrees and add all ingredients to a medium bowl. Pour inside baking pan or fill large muffin tin.

Bake for 30-40 minutes or until brown.

Inside will be moist so let cool for 10 minutes before serving.

Spicy Egg Cups

Ingredients:

3 eggs, beaten

One potato, baked and chopped small

One cup of salsa (any variety)

One cup of cheese (any variety, shredded)

Salt and pepper to taste

Directions:

Preheat oven to 375 degrees. Using a muffin tin, add one teaspoon of potatoes, followed by egg and salsa. Leave about a ¼ inch from the top.

When all cups are filled, place on baking sheet and let cook for 20 minutes.

Top with cheese and let sit in oven for an additional 5-10 minutes.

Serve with English muffin or slice in half and eat with pita bread or tortilla.

Spicy Egg Salad

Ingredients:

4-5 eggs, boiled and chopped small

One cup of hot mustard (any variety)

½ cup of green onion and celery, chopped fine

Two tablespoons of jalapeno relish (optional)

One (8 oz.) carton of plain yogurt

Directions:
In a large bowl, mix all ingredients together evenly and let chill for at least an hour before serving.

Spinach Cakes

Spinach cakes can be easily made using your muffin tins and oven. You can use either the frozen or fresh spinach depending upon the availability of time.

Ingredients:

1 (12 oz) can of frozen spinach, thawed and chopped

2 cups of Parmesan cheese, shredded

2 large eggs, beaten

Salt and Pepper, according to taste

1 clove of garlic, finely chopped

Directions:

You can easily make these delicious spinach cakes in an oven, using your muffin tins.

Preheat your oven to 400 degrees and coat your muffin tins with cooking spray.

It is important that your spinach is thawed at room temperature before you are preparing your spinach cakes.

Chop the spinach in a food processor. Add to a medium sized bowl and mix in all the ingredients until they are well incorporated into each other.

Divide the mixture into 8 to 10 muffin tins. Bake in a reheated oven for 15 to 20 minutes.

Let the muffin tins stand on a wire rack for at least 5 minutes before you start taking the spinach cakes out.

Serving Suggestions:

Serve with ore parmesan or any other cheese of your choice.

Spinach Mushroom Frittata

Ingredients:

5-6 eggs, beaten

One cup of spinach, fresh or frozen

½ cup of mushrooms, sliced

2 tablespoons of vegetable oil

Salt and pepper to taste

Directions:

Preheat oven to 375 degrees. Coat large pan in oil and add mushrooms, followed by spinach.

Stir enough for coverage and add one teaspoon of oil, if necessary.

Pour egg mixture to vegetables and let bake between 20-25 minutes.

Top with favorite cheese, if desired.

Sunrise Muffins

Ingredients:

One box of spiced cake mix

½ cup of carrots, shredded

½ cup of raisins (any variety)

½ cup of walnuts

One egg and oil (if directions call for it)

Directions:
Preheat oven to 375 degrees and prepare cake mix as directed.
Add remaining ingredients and mix evenly.
Use oil to coat muffin tin and pour mix inside each cup.
Bake for 30 minutes or until edges brown.

Super Onion Potatoes

Ingredients:

One box of dry onion soup

6-8 red or 5-6 russet potatoes, chopped

One large onion, sliced thin

One cup of vegetable oil

Directions:

Preheat oven to 400 degrees. Mix all ingredients (including both packets of soup) until even.

Place on a shallow baking sheet evenly. Let cook for 25-30 minutes or until edges are crisp.

Super Stuffed Eggs

Ingredients:

6 eggs, boiled and halved

One cup of imitation bacon bits

½ cup of green onions, chopped fine

One teaspoon of garlic, minced

½ cup of Dijon or spicy mustard

Directions:

In a large bowl, add yolks and all ingredients. Mix until fairly smooth and place one tablespoon inside each egg white. Refrigerate for at least one hour before serving.

Sweet-n-Spicy Greens

Ingredients:

Three cups of mixed greens (spinach, mustard, collard, etc.), fresh and chopped

One teaspoon of crushed red pepper

½ cup of sweet chili sauce

Two tablespoons of garlic olive oil

Directions:

Using a large pan, heat oil on medium and add greens. Stir, cover and let cook for five minutes.

Stir again and add sauce and peppers.

Let greens sit for 10 minutes before serving.

Tomato, Mozzarella and Basil on Flatbread

Tomato and basil combined with mozzarella cheese and a flatbread ,akes a very interesting combination that you are simply going to love.

Ingredients:

1 serving of flatbread makes 2 flatbreads

2 tablespoons of pesto sauce

½ cup tomato, thinly sliced

1 tablespoon of fresh basil leaves, finely chopped

¼ cup of mozzarella cheese, shredded

Directions:

Preheat your oven to 450 degrees and generously coat a baking dish with cooking spray.

Take one flatbread and spread the pesto sauce on it. Place a tomato on the top followed by a few basil leaves. In the end, sprinkle some Mozzarella on the top.

Bake in a preheated oven for about 5 minutes or until the cheese melts.

Vegetarian Enchiladas

Ingredients:

One dozen corn tortillas

One cup of zucchini, chopped small

One can (8 oz.) of vegetarian refried beans

One large onion, chopped small

One can (20 oz. Or more) of ranchero or enchilada sauce
Directions:
Preheat oven at 400 degrees and wrap tortillas in wet paper towel and cook in the microwave for one minute. Keep wrapped until ready to use. Mix zucchini, beans and onion in a medium bowl.
Using a casserole dish or baking sheet, place one tortilla flat and add 2-3 teaspoons of the vegetable mixture inside.
Roll placing open end down. Repeat with all tortillas.
Let cook for 30 minutes covered and add generous amount of sauce, followed by shredded cheese, if desired.

Veggie Enchilada Casserole

Casseroles make ta perfect breakfast on any morning. Since they are so much filling, they provide you with maximum energy to tackle with your everyday tasks.

Ingredients:

1 cup of onion, chopped

2 cups of zucchini, sliced

1 jar of Enchilada sauce

12 corn tortillas

2 cups of Monterey Jack cheese, shredded

Directions:

Preheat oven to 375 degrees and coat a 9x9 inch casserole dish with cooking spray.

Add oil in a skillet. Heat it a little bit and add in the onions. Sauté, and immediately add in the zucchini slices as well. Sauté until the onion and the zucchini Is tender.

Place a layer of the Enchilada sauce on the bottom of the casserole dish. Make a layer of 6 tortillas and spread another layer of sauce over it. Spoon out the vegetable mixture on the top and sprinkle half of the shredded cheese.

In the end, put another layer of tortillas followed by a layer of the Enchilada sauce and a last layer of the remaining cheese.

Bake in a preheated oven for 20 minutes or until the cheese melts.

Vegan Mexican Stew

If you are craving for something Mexican, then this vegan Mexican stew is a real delight to actually sensationalize your taste buds.

Don't forget to keep a glass of water with you, because it is really hot!

Ingredients:

2 ½ cups of potatoes, peeled and cubed

1 cup of carrots, chopped

4 cups of vegetable stock

1 tablespoon of chili powder

1 tablespoon of cumin seeds

Directions:

Add around 4 cups or more of water in a pot and add some salt in it. Add the potatoes and carrots in it and let them cook until they become a bit tender.

Drain the water and keep the vegetables aside.

Heat oil in a pan and sauté the half cooked potatoes and carrots in it. Add in the chili powder and season with some salt. Mix and let the vegetables cook for a few minutes. Add in the cumin seeds and cook again for a minute.

Add in the vegetable stock and give the vegetables a stir. Bring the stock to a boil and then turn down the flame to low. Let the stew simmer for 30 to 45 minutes.

Season with green chilies.

Zucchini Casserole

Ingredients:

3 zucchini squash, chopped small

One large onion, chopped small

One cup of instant rice (any variety)

Two tablespoons of Italian blend or all-purpose seasoning

Two cups of Italian Blend or mozzarella cheese, shredded
Directions:
Preheat oven at 350 degrees. Using a casserole dish or Dutch oven, mix all ingredients (except cheese) together.
Add one cup of water and mix again before placing inside oven, covered.
Let cook for 20 minutes and top with cheese, let cook for an additional 5-10 minutes.

Zucchini Patties

Zucchini patties are a light wonderful snack which you can enjoy with various variations of your own. Whether you want to eat them in simple form, without adding much of the other ingredients, or you want to experience having them with various additions, they always make a nice addition to your usual tea or coffee time. Addition of a nice dip and a fresh salad makes them an ideal meal.

Ingredients:

2 cups of zucchini, grated

2 whole eggs, slightly beaten

½ cup of all-purpose flour

¼ cup of onion

Salt, as per your taste

Directions:

Grate the zucchini using a grater or a food processor.

Take a medium sized bowl and mix all the ingredients together. Start making small patties out of them and shallow fry them over medium flame.

Serving Suggestions:

You can also make your own variation by adding cheese, green chilies and even tomatoes.

Vegetarian Salad Recipes

Fruit Salad Recipes

Apple Salad

It is a perfect and tasty salad that your family is sure to love.
Ingredients:
5 medium Granny Smith apples, cored and cubed into ½-inch size
Juice of 1 lemon
½ cup of mayonnaise
¼ cup of white sugar
½ cup of celery, sliced thinly
½ cup of golden raisins
½ cup of walnuts, chopped
Directions:
In a large bowl, add apples. Pour lemon juice over apples. Now add remaining ingredients and mix well.
Serving Suggestions:
You can add some whipped cream for more creamy touch.

Avocado & Fruit Salad

Make this easy, quick and nourishing salad to keep your lunch cool in summer.

Ingredients:

4 teaspoons of honey

¼ cup of lemon juice

¾ cup of papaya, peeled and cubed into ¾-inch size

¾ cup of pineapple, peeled and cubed into ¾-inch size

¾ cup of strawberries, halved

¾ cup of Mexican yam, cubed into ½-inch size

2 tablespoons of mint, chopped coarsely

1 small jalapeno, seeded and chopped finely

1 ripe avocado, peeled, pitted and cut into ¾-inch chunks

Directions:

In a bowl, add honey and lemon juice and whisk well. Add all fruits, mint and jalapeno and mix till coated well with lemonade dressing.

Now fold in avocado and serve.

Serving Suggestions:

You can also add fruit of your choice.

Citrus Salad

This colorful and gorgeous salad is great for breakfast as well as lunch and dinner.

Ingredients:

¼ cup of honey

¼ teaspoon of cardamom powder

2 tablespoons of lime juice

1 large grapefruit, peeled and sectioned

1 naval orange, peeled and sectioned

1 mandarin orange, peeled and sectioned

1 blood orange, peeled and sectioned

Directions:

In a small pan, add honey, cardamom and lime juice. Bring to a boil and simmer for 10 minutes. Remove from heat and keep aside to cool.

In a large bowl, add all fruits. Pour honey mixture on fruits and gently toss to coat well.

Chill before serving.

Serving Suggestions:

You can garnish your salad with toasted nuts.

Cranberry Salad

A heavenly tasty salad is always a big hit for special dinners.

Ingredients:

2 cups of fresh cranberries

2 cups of mixed salad green

½ cup of walnuts, toasted and chopped

4 ounces of feta cheese, crumbled

1 tablespoon of honey

2 tablespoons of balsamic vinegar

1 teaspoon of Dijon mustard

¼ teaspoon of black pepper

¼ cup of olive oil

Directions:

In a large bowl, add cranberries, greens, walnuts and cheese and mix.

In another bowl, add remaining ingredients and whisk till well blended. Pour vinaigrette on salad and toss to coat well.

Serving Suggestions:

You can substitute the walnuts with almonds or pecans.

Frozen Fruit Salad

This unique, refreshing and delicious salad is a cool treat….

Ingredients:

1 cup of mayonnaise

8 ounces of cream cheese

½ cup of cherries, quartered

1 (20-ounce) can of pineapples chunks, drained

2 bananas, sliced

2½ cups of miniature marshmallows

1 cup of almonds, chopped

½ cup of heavy cream, whipped

Lettuce leaves

Directions:

In a bowl, add mayonnaise and cream cheese and whisk till smooth. Add fruits, marshmallows and almonds and mix. Now fold in cream. Cover and freeze overnight.

Remove from refrigerator 10 minutes before serving. Cut into desired pieces and serve on lettuce-lined plates.

Serving Suggestions:

If you like tangy flavor then use sour cream instead of heavy cream.

Fruit Yogurt Salad

Ingredients:

I mango, peeled and cubed

1 banana, sliced

½ cup of fresh strawberries, sliced

½ cup of raspberries

½ cup of cherries, halved

½ cup of pineapple, cubed

½ cup of grapes

½ cup of plain yogurt

White sugar, to taste

Directions:

In a large bowl, add all fruit and mix. Add yogurt and mix to coat well. Sprinkle sugar on salad. Chill and serve.

Serving suggestions:

Swap the simple yogurt with flavored yogurt and this will bring a pleasant change in taste.

Grape Salad

It is a superb salad that will never fail to be a great hit.

Ingredients:

1 (8-ounce) package of cream cheese, softened

1/3 cup of white sugar

1 teaspoon of vanilla extract

1 cup of red seedless grapes

1 cup of green seedless grapes

1 cup of pecans, toasted and chopped

Brown sugar, for sprinkling

Directions:

In a bowl, add cream cheese, sugar and vanilla extract. Beat with an electric mixer till smooth.

Add grapes and mix gently till grapes are well coated. Sprinkle pecans and brown sugar on salad. Cover and refrigerate for 1 hour.

Serving Suggestions:

You can replace sugar with honey.

Mango Walnut Salad

An out of the world sweet and light summer salad...

Ingredients:

2 large mangoes, peeled and cubed

1 bunch of baby spinach, torn

2 tablespoons of olive oil

3 tablespoons of white vinegar

3 tablespoons of balsamic vinegar

¼ teaspoon of fresh tarragon, chopped

2 teaspoons of dry mustard

Salt and black pepper, to taste

¾ cup of toasted walnuts

Directions:

In a large bowl, mix mangoes and spinach. In another bowl, add oil, white vinegar, balsamic vinegar, tarragon, mustard, salt and black pepper and mix till blended.

Pour vinaigrette on salad and toss to coat well. Sprinkle walnuts on top and serve.

Serving Suggestions:

You can serve this salad with sugar free raspberry vinaigrette.

Ambrosia Salad

Amazing stuff!!! Surely it is a crowd pleasing salad.

Ingredients:

1 (8-ounce) can of fruit cocktail, drained well
1 (10-ounce) can of peaches, drained well
1 (8-ounce) can of pineapple, drained well
1 (10-ounce) jar of maraschino cherries, drained well
1 (8-ounce) can of frozen whipped toping, thawed
½ cup of walnuts, chopped
2 cups of coconut flakes, shredded
1½ cups of miniature colorful marshmallows
1½ cups of white marshmallows
1 teaspoon of cinnamon powder
1 teaspoon of nutmeg powder

Directions:

In a large bowl, add all ingredients and mix completely. Chill before serving.

Serving Suggestions:

You can use seasonal fresh fruits instead of canned fruits.

Watermelon Feta Salad

This sweet and salty summer salad is just wonderful and refreshing.

Ingredients:

¼ cup of balsamic vinegar

¼ cup of extra-virgin olive oil

Salt and black pepper, to taste

2 tablespoons of fresh mint, chopped finely

1 pound watermelon, seeded and cut into small chunks

1 small sweet onion, sliced into rings

4 ounces of feta cheese, crumbled

Mint sprigs, for garnishing

Directions:

In a small bowl, add vinegar, oil, salt and pepper. Whisk till well blended. Stir in chopped mint. Keep aside.

In a large mixing bowl, add watermelon, onion and cheese and mix. Pour vinaigrette on salad. Toss to coat well.

While serving, garnish with mint sprigs.

Serving Suggestions:

Serve this refreshing salad as a side dish with grilled vegetables.

Coconut & Avocado Salad

The combination of avocado and apple with honey yogurt makes a great tasty snack.

Ingredients:

1 ripe avocado, peeled, pitted and diced

1 cup of coconut flakes

1 large red apple, cored and diced

½ cup of almonds, slivered

3 tablespoons of honey

3 tablespoons of vanilla yogurt

1 cup of frozen blueberries, thawed

Directions:

In a large bowl, add avocado, coconut, apples and almonds and toss. In another bowl, mix honey and yogurt.

Pour honey dressing on salad. Stir to coat well. Fold in blueberries. Refrigerate to chill.

Serving Suggestions:

You can use some lime juice to give tangy flavor to dressing.

Pumpkin & Apple Salad

This tasty and refreshing salad is easy and quick to make recipe.

Ingredients:

For Dressing:

4 tablespoons of walnut oil

1 tablespoon of sweet grainy mustard

Juice of 1 lemon

2 tablespoons of maple syrup

1 tablespoon of fresh ginger, grated

A pinch of salt and pepper

For Salad:

1½ cups of red apples, peeled and grated

1½ cups of pumpkin, peeled and grated

¼ cup of walnuts, chopped, divided

¼ cup of raisins

Radicchio leaves, washed, pat dried and separated

Directions:

In a bowl add all dressing ingredients and mix well. In a large bowl, add apples, pumpkin, half of walnuts and raisins. Toss well. Pour dressing on salad and mix till well combined.

In a serving plate, place a radicchio leaf. Place salad on each leaf. Garnish with remaining walnuts and serve.

Serving Suggestions:

This salad will be a nice partner of veggie burgers.

Mandarin Orange Salad

Awesome salad!! This is a really yummy green salad in which oranges and almonds give a great twist.

Ingredients:

1 tablespoon of balsamic vinegar

1 tablespoon of extra-virgin olive oil

1 tablespoon of orange juice

¼ teaspoon of dry mustard

1 teaspoon of sugar

6 cups of mixed salad greens

1 (10-ounce) can of mandarin oranges, peeled and sectioned

½ cup of fresh raspberries

¼ cup of almonds, toasted and sliced

Directions:

In a small bowl, add vinegar, oil, orange juice, mustard and sugar. Whisk till well combined.

In a large bowl, place greens, oranges and raspberries.

Pour dressing on salad. Toss gently till well coated. Top with almonds.

Serving Suggestions:

You can serve this salad on bed of lettuce for a nice touch.

Asparagus & Berry Salad

Prepare this refreshing salad in summer as a light evening meal for your family.

Ingredients:

1 pound of fresh asparagus, trimmed and cut into 1-inch pieces

3 tablespoons of extra-virgin olive oil, divided

Salt and black pepper, to taste

½ teaspoon of sugar

2 tablespoons of balsamic vinegar

3 cups of fresh strawberries, sliced

½ medium red onion, sliced thinly

8 cups of mixed salad greens

½ cup of walnuts, toasted and chopped

Directions:

Preheat oven to 400 degrees F. Grease a baking dish. In a bowl, add asparagus, 2 tablespoons of oil, salt and black pepper and toss well.

Spread asparagus in prepared baking dish. Bake for 15 to 20 minutes or till it become tender.

In a small bowl, add sugar, vinegar and remaining oil and whisk well. In a large serving bowl, add asparagus, strawberries, onion, greens and walnuts and mix.

Pour vinaigrette on salad and toss to coat well.

Serving Suggestions:

Enjoy this salad with breadsticks for more crunch.

Cherry Cheddar Waldorf Salad

Apples, cherries and nuts offer a great crunchy flavor to this simple but delicious salad.

Ingredients:

2 large golden apples, cored and chopped

1 tablespoon of lemon juice

1 cup of fresh cherries, pitted

½ cup of dried cranberries

2 celery ribs, chopped

½ cup of almonds, toasted and slivered

¼ cup of raisins

2 tablespoons of honey

¼ cup of sour cream

¼ cup of mayonnaise

¼ cup of cheddar cheese, shredded

Directions:

In a bowl add apples. Sprinkle lemon juice on apples. Now, add cherries, cranberries, celery and almonds and toss.

In another bowl, add honey, sour cream and mayonnaise and whisk till well mixed. Pour dressing on salad and mix to coat well.

Top with cheddar cheese. Chill before serving.

Serving Suggestions:

You can add mini marshmallows for extra unique flavor.

Pasta Salad Recipes

Angel Hair Pasta Salad

A unique and great to make salad that can be expanded to feed all family.

Ingredients:

1 pound of angel hair pasta

½ cup of olive oil

4 cloves of garlic, minced

Salt and black pepper, to taste

¾ cup of Parmesan cheese, shredded and divided

¾ cup of mozzarella cheese, shredded

4 tomatoes, seeded and cubed

1 cup of fresh basil leaves, chopped

¼ cup of pine nuts, toasted and chopped

Directions:

Boil pasta according to package directions. Drain and place into a large bowl.

While pasta is boiling, add oil in a small pan. Heat the oil on medium-low heat. Sauté garlic for 2 to 3 minutes. Pour garlic and oil on warm pasta and mix.

Stir in salt, black pepper, half of Parmesan cheese and mozzarella cheese.

While serving, add tomatoes, basil, pine nuts and remaining Parmesan cheese to pasta and mix well.

Serving Suggestions:

 For more refreshing taste, serve with lime wedges.

Cucumber, Tomato & Shell Pasta Salad

A nice Italian dressing adds a lot of zip in this fresh salad.

Ingredients:
1 pound of shell pasta, cooked according to package directions
1 cucumber, cut into bite-size pieces
2 tomatoes cut into bite-size pieces
4 tablespoons of salad seasoning
1 (16-ounce) jar of Italian dressing
Directions:
In a large bowl, add pasta, cucumber and tomatoes and toss. Add seasoning and dressing and mix till well coated. Cover and refrigerate to chill.
Serving Suggestions:
Serve this refreshing salad with pizza of your choice.

Artichoke Pasta Salad

This is an easy and fabulous salad.
Ingredients:
1 (6 ½ -ounce) jar of marinated artichoke hearts
1 cup of bow tie pasta, cooked according to package directions
1 cup of black olives, pitted
1 cup of cherry tomatoes, halved
½ cups of mushrooms, sliced finely
1 tablespoon of fresh parsley, chopped
½ teaspoon f dried oregano
½ teaspoon of dried basil
2 small cloves of garlic, minced
Salt and black pepper, to taste
Directions:
In a large bowl, add all ingredients and toss well. Refrigerate for 3 to 4 hours.
Serving Suggestions:

This salad will be wonderful with a burger.

Black Bean Pasta Salad

This tasty salad will be a popular hit for potlucks.

Ingredients:

¼ cup of olive oil

Juice of 1 lime

3 small cloves of garlic, minced

1½ cups of elbow macaroni, cooked according to package directions

2 cans of black beans, drained and rinsed

2 pounds of fresh roma tomatoes, seeded and diced

2 teaspoons of Tabasco sauce

Salt, to taste

2 teaspoons of cumin powder

1 teaspoon of dried oregano

8-ounces of feta cheese, crumbled

½ cup of fresh cilantro, chopped

Directions:

In a large serving bowl, add all ingredients except cilantro. Mix till well combined. Garnish salad with cilantro and serve.

Serving Suggestions:

Serve this pasta with margarita.

Spinach & Pasta Salad

A unique and healthy salad packed with iron.

Ingredients:

 1 (16-ounce) package of bow tie pasta, cooked according to package directions

2 cups of fresh basil leaves, chopped

1o-ounces of spinach leaves, torn

1 red onion, chopped

2 small cloves of garlic, minced

Juice of 1 lemon

Salt and black pepper, to taste

¾ cup of Parmesan cheese, grated

½ cup of walnuts, toasted

Directions

In a large serving bowl, add all ingredients except cheese and walnuts.

Toss to combine well. While serving, top with cheese and walnuts.

Serving Suggestions:

This salad has a perfect pairing with bean burger.

Creamy Italian Pasta Salad

A perfect salad for buffet….

Ingredients:

For Salad:

1 (12-ounce) package corkscrew pasta, cooked according to package directions

½ red bell pepper, chopped

½ green bell pepper, chopped

5 scallions, chopped finely

2 tablespoons of fresh parsley, chopped

3 cups of mozzarella cheese, shredded

6 eggs, hard boiled and chopped

For Dressing:

¼ cup of balsamic vinegar

1½ cups of mayonnaise

Salt and black pepper, to taste

1 teaspoon of dried oregano

Directions:

In a large serving bowl, add all salad ingredients and mix.

In another bowl, add all dressing ingredients and mix well.

Pour dressing on salad. Toss to coat well. Chill before serving.

Serving Suggestions:

You can replace with the vegetables of your choice.

Honey Mustard Macaroni Salad

This fabulous and yummy macaroni salad has the sweet and tangy flavor of honey mustard.

Ingredients:

For Macaroni Salad:

2 cups of elbow macaroni, cooked according to package directions

½ cup of red onion, chopped

1 medium cucumber, peeled and chopped coarsely

2 tablespoons of fresh parsley, minced

2 tablespoons of red peppers, roasted

For Dressing:

1 tablespoon of extra-virgin olive oil

1½ cups of apple cider vinegar

½ cup of prepared honey mustard

4 cloves of garlic, minced

Salt and black pepper, to taste

¼ teaspoon of red pepper flakes

Directions:

In a large bowl, add all salad ingredients and mix.

In another bowl, add all dressing ingredients. Whisk till blended completely. Pour dressing on salad and toss to coat well.

Cover and chill completely.

Serving Suggestions:

Enjoy this yummy salad with baked potatoes.

Tortellini Pasta Salad

This salad is super easy to make and always such a hit.

Ingredients:

1 (16-ounces) package of tortellini pasta, cooked according to package directions

1 green bell pepper, seeded and diced

1 red bell pepper, seeded and diced

1 red onion, diced

1 cup of creamy Caesar salad dressing

1 cup of Italian dressing

1 cup of Parmesan cheese, grated

Directions:

In a large salad bowl, add all ingredients and mix well. Refrigerate to chill before serving.

Serving Suggestions:

This easy salad goes well with any veggie meal.

Apple & Spinach Pasta Salad

A refreshing springtime pasta salad is perfect for celebrations.

Ingredients:

4 cups of penne pasta, cooked according to package directions

1 cup of baby spinach, torn

2 red apples, cored and diced

4 scallions, sliced thinly

¼ cup of almonds, toasted and chopped

½ cup of feta cheese, crumbled

1 tablespoon of extra-virgin olive oil

¼ cup of balsamic vinegar

Salt and black pepper, to taste

Directions:

In a large salad bowl, add pasta, spinach, apples, scallions, almonds and cheese and mix.

In another small bowl, whisk together oil, vinegar, salt and black pepper.

Pour vinaigrette on salad and toss to coat well.

Serving Suggestions:

This would be a dinner salad with a thick slice of Dakota on side.

Garden Vegetable Pasta Salad

A zesty salad with pasta and lots of crunchy vegetables.....

Ingredients:

For Salad:

2 cups of tri-colored pasta, cooked according to package directions

½ cup of olives, sliced

2 medium carrots, sliced thinly

1 green bell pepper, seeded and diced

1 red bell pepper, seeded and diced

2 tablespoons of canned peas, drained

2 roma tomatoes, chopped

1 red onion chopped

2 scallions, chopped

For Vinaigrette:

2 tablespoons of balsamic vinegar

4 tablespoons of extra-virgin olive oil

1 teaspoon of Dijon mustard

1 teaspoon of sugar

1 teaspoon of garlic, minced

1 teaspoon of fresh tarragon, chopped

2 teaspoons of fresh parsley

Salt and black pepper, to taste

Directions:

In a large salad bowl, mix pasta and vegetables. In a small bowl, mix vinaigrette ingredients till well combined.

Pour vinaigrette on salad and toss to coat well. Cover and refrigerate for 1 to 2 hours.

Serving Suggestions:

Tomato & Feta Pasta Salad

This pasta salad looks delicious and flavorful.

Ingredients:

2 cups of rotini pasta, cooked according to package directions

2 tablespoons of sweet onion, chopped

¼ cup of balsamic vinegar

1 tablespoon of extra-virgin olive oil

1 tomato, diced

¾ cup of feta cheese, crumbled

Salt and black pepper, to taste

¼ cup of fresh basil leaves, chopped

Directions:

In a bowl, add pasta, onion and vinegar and toss. Cover and refrigerate for 15 minutes.

Then add oil and toss well. While serving, add tomatoes and feta cheese.

Season with salt and black pepper. Garnish with basil leaves

Serving Suggestions:

This salad is perfect as a side for sandwich.

Sun Dried Tomato Pasta Salad

This is the salad that is prepared quickly and looks beautiful.
Ingredients:
2 tablespoons of olive oil
5 cloves of garlic, chopped finely
2 cups of spiral pasta, cooked according to package directions
1 cup of oil packed sun dried tomatoes, drained and sliced
Salt and black pepper, to taste
1 cup of fresh basil leaves, chopped finely
½ cup of Parmesan cheese, grated and divided
1 tablespoon of reserved sun-dried tomato oil
Directions:
In a pan, heat oil on medium heat. Sauté garlic for 2 minutes or till fragrant.
In a large bowl, add pasta, garlic with oil, tomatoes, salt, black pepper, basil and half of cheese. Mix to coat well.
Sprinkle half of cheese on top. Drizzle sun-dried tomato oil. Refrigerate for 4 to 5 hours.
Serving Suggestions:
Serve this beautiful pasta with toasted crunchy bread.

Coleslaw Fettuccini Salad

A mixture of coleslaw and pasta combined with delicious dressing creates a wonderful salad.

Ingredients:

8-ounces of fettuccine, cooked according to package directions

4 cup of broccoli, chopped finely

2 cups of green cabbage, chopped finely

2 cups of purple cabbage, chopped finely

2 cups of carrots, shredded

4 celery ribs, chopped finely

¼ cup of cider vinegar

2/3 cup of milk

2 cups of miracle whip

1 cup of sugar

½ cup of butter

2 (3-ounce) packages of ramen noodles with seasoning, broken

¼ cup of sesame seeds

2 tablespoons of almonds, slivered and sliced

Directions:

In a large bowl, add fettuccini and all vegetables and mix well.

In another bowl, add vinegar, milk, whip and sugar. Whisk till well blended. Pour dressing on salad and toss to coat well. Cover and refrigerate for 1 to 2 hours.

In a pan, melt butter on medium heat. Add ramen noodles with seasoning, sesame seed and almonds. Sauté till light brown. Let it cool.

Just before serving, mix ramen mixture in salad.

Serving Suggestions:

Enjoy this yummy salad with fries.

Pasta Salad

An excellent and refreshing pasta salad!!!

Ingredients:

2 cups of spiral pasta, cooked according to package directions

1 (2 ¼-ounce) can of black olives, chopped

1 cup of roma tomatoes, sliced

1 cucumber, seeded and diced

1 red bell pepper, seeded and diced

1 green bell pepper, seeded and diced

1 (16-ounce) jar of Italian salad dressing

6 tablespoons of salad seasoning

Directions:

In a large bowl, add pasta, olives, tomatoes, cucumber and bell peppers and mix.

In another small bowl, add salad dressing and seasoning and whisk till well combined. Pour dressing on salad.

Toss to coat well. Refrigerate to chill completely.

Serving suggestions:

Serve with chips of your choice.

Corkscrew Pasta Salad with Pecans & Slivered Almonds

This salad will be quite nice for potlucks or picnics.
Ingredients:

For Pasta Salad:
2½ cups of corkscrew pasta, cooked according to package directions
1 cup of cherry tomatoes
½ large onion, sliced thinly
¾ cup of kalamata olives, pitted and halved
1 cup fresh baby spinach, torn
¼ cup of pecans, toasted
½ cup of almonds, slivered and toasted
½ cup of feta cheese, crumbled
1 tablespoon of fresh basil eaves, chopped, for garnishing
For Dressing:
¼ cup of extra-virgin olive oil
3 tablespoons of water
3 tablespoons of lemon juice
1 tablespoon of dried parsley flakes
Salt and black pepper, to taste
Directions:
In a large bowl, add pasta and vegetables. Mix well.
In another bowl, add dressing ingredients and whisk till well combined. Pour dressing on salad and toss to coat well.
Top with pecans, almonds and feta cheese. Garnish with basil leaves.
Serving Suggestions:
You can use some Parmesan cheese for creamy touch.

Green Salad Recipes

Italian Salad

This salad is so simple, refreshing and tempting.

Ingredients:

For Salad:

2 cups of romaine lettuce, torn

1 cup of red leaf lettuce, torn

1 cup of radicchio, torn

1 cup of escarole, torn

½ green bell pepper, sliced

½ red bell pepper, sliced

12 cherry tomatoes

¼ cup of scallions, chopped finely

For Vinaigrette:

¼ cup of balsamic vinegar

¼ cup of grape seed oil

2 tablespoons of lemon juice

2 tablespoons of fresh basil leaves, chopped finely

Salt and black pepper powder, to taste

Directions:

In a large salad bowl, add all salad ingredients and mix.

In another bowl, add vinaigrette ingredients and whisk till well blended.

Pour vinaigrette on salad and toss to coat well. Serve immediately.

Serving Suggestions:

Serve with toasted and buttered Italian bread.

Winter Salad

This wonderful salad would be a welcome addition to any Thanksgiving or Christmas dinner.

Ingredients:

4 cups of quinoa, cooked and fluffed

½ radish, sliced thinly

½ medium red onion, sliced thinly

½ cup of dried cranberries

¼ cup of fresh mint leaves

3 tablespoons of balsamic vinegar

3 tablespoons of extra-virgin olive oil

¼ cup of feta cheese, crumbled

Salt and black pepper, to taste

Directions:

In a large salad bowl, add all ingredients. Toss to coat well. Serve immediately.

Serving suggestions:

You can top this winter salad with toasted nuts.

Blue Cheese Salad

This great salad is a good pick for when you want something different.

Ingredients:

4 cups of romaine lettuce, torn

1 small avocado, chopped

1 large apple, cored and chopped

½ cup of red onion, chopped

1/3 cup of blue cheese, mashed

8-ounces of plain yogurt

1 teaspoon of Dijon mustard

2 tablespoons of vinegar

1/3 cup of orange juice

¼ cup of walnuts, toasted and sliced

Directions:

In a large salad bowl, add lettuce, avocado, apple and onion and mix. In another bowl, add cheese, yogurt, mustard, vinegar and orange juice.

Mix to combine well. Add cheese dressing on salad and mix well. Top with walnuts.

Serving Suggestions:

You can add seasonal vegetables and fruits of your choice.

Greek Tossed Salad

This classic Greek salad gets a crunchy boost from fresh vegetables.

Ingredients:

For Salad:

15 kalamata olives

½ green bell pepper, sliced thinly

3 tomatoes, sliced into wedges

¼ red onion, sliced thinly into rings

½ cucumber, halved and sliced

4-ounces feta cheese, crumbled

For Dressing:

3 tablespoons of extra-virgin olive oil

1 small clove of garlic, minced

1½ tablespoons of fresh lemon juice

½ teaspoon of dried oregano

Salt and black pepper powder, to taste

Directions:

In a large bowl, add all salad ingredients and mix.

In another bowl, add dressing ingredients. Whisk well till well mixed.

While serving, pour dressing on salad. Toss to coat well.

Serving suggestions:

This fresh salad can be served as a side dish with traditional Greek veggie meal.

Walnut & Apple Salad

This is a sophisticated salad to be served with autumn meal.

Ingredients:

2 red apples, cored and sliced finely

8 cups of mixed salad greens, torn

¼ cup of balsamic vinegar

¼ cup of raisins

1 cup of red onion, chopped

1 tablespoon of Dijon mustard

White sugar, to taste

Salt and black pepper, to taste

1 cup of extra-virgin olive oil

½ cup of walnuts, toasted and chopped

Directions:

In a large bowl, add apples and salad greens and mix.

In a blender, add remaining ingredients except oil and walnuts. Puree till well mixed.

While processor is running, add oil in batches. Now puree till smooth.

Pour dressing on salad and toss to coat well. Top with walnuts and serve.

Serving Suggestions:

You can enhance the flavor by adding caramelized apples instead of simple apples.

Cucumber & Tomato Salad

This salad is wonderful to serve fully chilled on a hot summer lunch.

Ingredients:

¼ cup of balsamic vinegar

½ tablespoon of white sugar

Salt, to taste

2 medium cucumbers, peeled, seeded and sliced into ½-inch pieces

½ cup of fresh mint leaves, chopped

2 large ripe tomatoes, seeded and chopped

½ cup of red onion, chopped

2 tablespoons of olive oil

Black pepper, to taste

Serving suggestions:

In a small bowl, add vinegar, sugar, ½ teaspoon of salt and cucumber and mix. Keep aside for 1 hour.

In a salad bowl, add remaining ingredients. Mix in marinated cucumber.

Sprinkle desired salt and black pepper. Toss well to coat.

Serving Suggestions:

Enjoy this refreshing salad with baked potatoes.

Mango, Pineapple & Kale Salad

A colorful and sweet salad for a light brunch…..
Ingredients:
For Salad:
1 cup of mango, peeled and chopped
½ cup of fresh pineapple chunks, chopped
5 cups of kale, removed stems and torn
1 tablespoon of dried coconut, grated
1 cup of pecans, toasted and chopped
For Dressing:
¾ cup of coconut milk
¼ cup of fresh lime juice
1 tablespoon of coconut oil, melted
1 cup of pineapple chunks
Salt, to taste
Directions:
In a salad bowl, add all salad ingredients except pecans.
In a food processor, add all dressing ingredients. Puree till smooth.
Pour dressing on salad and toss to coat well.
Just before serving, garnish with pecans.
Serving Suggestions:
This salad is a great hit with pineapple juice.

Baby Arugula & Avocado Salad

Here is healthy and beautiful salad that will impress your family.
Ingredients:
For Salad:
2 cups of baby arugula,
1 ripe avocado, peeled, pitted and chopped
1 medium tomato, chopped
3 tablespoons of Parmesan cheese, grated
For Vinaigrette:
1½ tablespoon of balsamic vinegar
2 tablespoons of extra-virgin olive oil
2 tablespoons of water
2 teaspoons of white sugar
2 tablespoons of fresh cilantro, chopped finely
Salt and black pepper, to taste
Directions:
In a large bowl, add all salad ingredients except cheese and mix.
In another bowl, add all dressing ingredients. Whisk till well combined. Pour vinaigrette on salad.
Toss to coat well. Sprinkle Parmesan cheese on top and serve.
Serving Suggestions:
This salad is great if served with grilled bread.

Portobello & Spinach Salad

The crunchy flavor of spinach with mushrooms and creamy dressing makes this a savory salad to please all plates.

Ingredients:

1/3 cup of extra-virgin olive oil, divided

1 (6-ounce) package of Portobello mushrooms, sliced

1 cup of fresh spinach, torn

10 grape tomatoes, halved

1 small red onion, sliced thinly

2 tablespoons of balsamic vinegar

2 tablespoons of mayonnaise

½ teaspoon of white sugar

1 clove of garlic, minced

Salt and black pepper, to taste

Directions:

In a pan, heat 1 tablespoon of oil on medium heat. Sauté mushrooms for 4 to 5 minutes. Transfer mushrooms to a bowl and let it cool.

Then, add vegetables in bowl and mix. In another bowl, add remaining oil, vinegar, mayonnaise, sugar, garlic, salt and black pepper.

Whisk till well combined and smooth. Pour dressing on salad and toss to coat well.

Serving Suggestions:

Apple, Orange & Spinach Salad

It's a quick, tasty and eye-catching salad.

Ingredients:

2 tablespoons of extra-virgin olive oil

Juice of 1 orange

2 apples, cored and chopped

3 dried dates, chopped

1 orange, peeled, removed stems and cut into chunks

1 bunch of fresh spinach, torn

Salt and black pepper, to taste

Directions:

In a small bowl, whisk together oil and orange juice.

Place apple slices in it and keep aside. In a large bowl, add remaining ingredients.

Add in apple with oil and juice. Toss to coat well. Serve immediately.

Serving Suggestions:

You can garnish with some crumbled feta cheese to add the flavor.

Pear & Pecan Salad

This elegant salad can be made in minutes to accompany your meals.

Ingredients:

For Dressing:

½ cup of mayonnaise

¼ cup of maple syrup

1/3 cup of apple cider vinegar

2 tablespoons of brown sugar

Salt and black pepper, to taste

¼ cup of walnut oil

For Salad:

1 large pear, cored and sliced

½ cup of red onion, sliced thinly

2 cups of mixed salad greens

½ cup of blue cheese, crumbled

½ cup of pecans, toasted, chopped and divided

Directions:

In a food processor, add all ingredients except oil. Pulse till well mixed.

While, motor running, add oil slowly. Pulse till mixture becomes smooth. Keep aside.

In a large salad bowl, add all salad ingredients and half of pecans. Pour dressing on salad and toss to coat well. Top with remaining pecans.

Serving Suggestions:

You can substitute honey with maple syrup.

Grapefruit & Avocado Salad

An eye-catching salad with wonderful combination of flavors!!

Ingredients:

4 tablespoons of extra-virgin olive oil

Juice of 1 lemon

1 teaspoon of honey

Salt and black pepper, to taste

3 pink grapefruits, peeled and sectioned

2 ripe avocado, peeled, pitted and diced

Directions:

In a small bowl, add oil, lemon juice, honey, salt and black pepper. Whisk till well blended.

In a large bowl, add grapefruit and avocado. Pour dressing on salad and toss to coat well.

Serving Suggestions:

This salad is tastes good with tortilla soup.

Asparagus Salad

This delicious salad is a perfect side dish in spring meals.

Ingredients:

1½ pounds of fresh asparagus, trimmed

¼ cup of cider vinegar

¼ cup f extra-virgin olive oil

½ tablespoon of Dijon mustard

¼ teaspoon of sugar

Salt and black pepper, to taste

3 scallions, sliced thinly

Directions:

In a pan, add small amount of water and boil. Cook asparagus for about 6 minutes or till crisp tender. Drain completely. Add in a bowl and cover.

Refrigerate for 1 to 1½ hours. In a small bowl, add remaining ingredients except scallions and whisk till well mixed. Keep aside for at least 1 hour.

Then in a salad bowl, add asparagus and scallions. Pour dressing on salad. Toss to coat well.

Serving Suggestions:

Enjoy this delicious salad by serving it paired with poached eggs.

Tomato & Zucchini Salad

This fresh veggie salad is a big hit for summer dinners.
Ingredients:
For Vinaigrette:
¼ cup of balsamic vinegar
¼ cup of extra-virgin olive oil
3 tablespoons of water
1 teaspoon of dried basil
2 cloves of garlic, minced
Salt and black pepper, to taste
For Salad:
1 large zucchini, cut into chunks
2 ripe tomatoes, cut into chunks
½ red bell pepper, diced
½ green bell pepper, diced
½ sweet onion, chopped
Directions:
In a bowl, add all vinaigrette ingredients and whisk till well combined. Keep aside.
In a large bowl add all salad ingredients. Pour vinaigrette on salad.
Toss to coat well. Let it cool for 1 hour in refrigerator.
Serving Suggestions:
You can add ½ teaspoon of grated lemon zest to brighten the flavor.

Apple & pumpkin Salad

This is very refreshing salad, is easy and fast to make.
Ingredients:
For Salad:
1½ cups of pumpkin, peeled, seeded and grated
3 apples, peeled and grated
¼ cup of walnuts, toasted and chopped
½ cup of raisins
For Dressing:
3 tablespoons of walnut oil
1 tablespoon of maple syrup
Juice of 1 lemon
1 tablespoon of fresh ginger, grated
1 tablespoon of mild mustard
Salt and black pepper, to taste
Directions:
In a salad bowl, add pumpkin, apples, walnuts and raisins and mix.
In another small bowl, add all dressing ingredients. Whisk till well combined.
Pour dressing on salad. Toss to coat well.
Serving Suggestions:
You can serve this refreshing salad on lettuce leaves for a nice presentation.

Lentil & Chard Salad

This lentil chard salad will be a huge hit for special occasions.
Ingredients:
¾ cup of lentils, uncooked
3 cups of Swiss chard leaves, removed stems and chopped coarsely
Salt and black pepper, to taste
2 tablespoons of extra-virgin olive oil
1 tablespoon of lemon juice
3 scallions, chopped very finely
½ cup of feta cheese, crumbled2 large tomatoes, chopped
Directions:
Add lentils in water filled pan. Bring to a boil on medium-high heat. Cook lentils for 15 to 20 minutes. Drain well.
Add lentils into a large bowl. Add chard leaves in bowl and toss well with warm lentils till chard leaves wilt a little. Sprinkle some salt.
In another bowl, add salt, black pepper, oil, lemon juice and scallions.
Whisk till well mixed. Add tomatoes in bowl. Pour dressing on lentil mixture and toss to coat well.
Just before serving, top salad with cheese.
Serving Suggestions:
Enjoy your salad with toasted and buttered bread.

Walnut & Raisins Salad

A light and beautiful addition to your dinning table…..
Ingredients:
4 cups of baby spinach, torn
¾ cup of walnuts, toasted and chopped
½ cup of golden raisins
¼ cup of extra-virgin olive oil
¼ cup of balsamic vinegar
¼ cup of orange juice
Salt and black pepper, to taste
2 tablespoons of brown sugar
¼ cup of Parmesan cheese, grated freshly
Directions:
In a large salad bowl, add spinach, walnuts and raisins.
In another small bowl, add remaining ingredients except cheese.
Whisk till well combined.
Pour dressing on salad and toss to coat well. Top with Parmesan cheese.
Serving Suggestions:
You can replace mixed salad greens or chard leaves with baby spinach.

Summer Rice Salad

This elegant summer salad is also great to take to picnics.

Ingredients:

1½ cups of brown rice, cooked

1 (15-ounce) can of kidney beans, rinsed and drained

¼ cup of broccoli florets, cut into bite size pieces

¼ cup of yellow bell pepper, chopped

¼ cup of red bell pepper, chopped

¼ cup of green bell pepper, chopped

¼ cup of red onion, chopped

Black pepper, to taste

1 tablespoon of extra-virgin olive oil

2 tablespoons of Italian seasoning

2 tablespoons of almonds, toasted

Directions:

In a large bowl, add rice and vegetables. Sprinkle black pepper. Add oil and dressing in bowl. Toss to coat well.

Sprinkle almonds on top. Refrigerate for at least 1 to 2 hours before serving.

Serving Suggestions:

This salad has a great pairing with tortilla chips.

Catalina Parmesan Salad

It is a super simple and easy salad.

Ingredients:

1 cup of tomatoes, chopped

2 cups of romaine lettuce leaves, torn

¼ cup of Catalina salad dressing

¼ cup of Parmesan cheese, grated freshly

Directions:

In a salad bowl, add tomatoes, lettuce and dressing. Toss to coat well. Sprinkle cheese on top.

Serving Suggestions:

This salad will go nice with grilled vegetables.

Butternut Squash Salad

Make this beautiful and delicious salad and surely it will be moved in your recipe folder.

Ingredients:

1 small butternut squash, peeled, seeded and cut into ¾-inch pieces

3 tablespoons of extra-virgin olive oil, divided

Salt and black pepper powder, to taste

4 cups of romaine lettuce, torn

¼ cup of kalamata olives, pitted and halved

1 (15½-ounce) can of chickpeas, rinsed

1 Granny Smith apple, cored and sliced

¼ cup of balsamic vinegar

2 tablespoons of fresh dill

4-ounces of feta cheese, crumbled

Directions:

Preheat oven to 450 degrees F. Line a baking dish with wax paper. Place butternut squash pieces on baking dish. Drizzle oil on butternut squash. Sprinkle some salt and black pepper. Roast butternut squash pieces for 25 to 30 minutes. Keep aside to cool completely.

After cooling, add butternut squash in a large salad bowl. Add lettuce, olives, chickpeas and apples in the bowl. In another bowl, add remaining oil, vinegar, dill, and desired salt and black pepper. Whisk till well combined.

Pour vinaigrette on salad and toss to coat well. Top with feta cheese.

Serving Suggestions:

You will love to eat this salad with harissa soup.

Vegetarian Side Dish Recipes

Bite Sized Appetizers and Sides

Hot Cheddar Corn Bites

Ingredients:

One package of corn bread

One small can of corn, drained

One egg

½ cup of milk

One cup of cheddar cheese, chopped small

Two cups of vegetable oil

Directions:
Heat oil on medium using a large pot or Dutch oven. Mix all ingredients in a large bowl until evenly mixed together.
Using a ladle or tablespoon, take a hefty scoop of mixture and place inside oil. Turn after it rises for even cooking. Cook each drop for no more than 10 minutes
Drain on paper towel and let cool before eating.

Hot Jack Poppers

Ingredients:

One box of cornbread mix

10-12 large jalapeno peppers

One cup of pepper jack cheese, cubed small

Two cups of vegetable oil
Directions:
Fill large pan or Dutch oven with oil and heat on medium.
Prepare mix according to instructions inside a medium bowl.
Make a lengthwise slit in each pepper and fill with 2-3 cheese cubes. Once they are all filled, dip in mixture, then place in oil.
Cook for no more than 10 minutes, turning constantly. Let drain on paper towel and cool for five minutes before serving.

Lettuce Wraps

Ingredients:

6-8 lettuce leaves (Romaine, Iceberg, Green or Red)

2-3 avocados, chopped small

One cup of imitation bacon bits

One can (8 oz.) of tomatoes, chopped and drained

2 green onions, chopped fine

Two tablespoons of plain yogurt

One tablespoon of garlic, minced

Salt and pepper to taste

Directions:
Mix avocadoes, bacon, tomatoes and onions together until even. Add yogurt and garlic, followed by salt and pepper and blend well.
Mixture should be slightly chunky before adding to inside of lettuce leaves.
Place one tablespoon at the edge of leaf and roll lengthwise. Secure with toothpick, if needed.

Spinach Puffs

Ingredients:

One cup of frozen spinach, thawed

One package of Filo pastry

½ cup of imitation bacon bits (optional)

One can of mushroom soup, creamed

Salt and pepper to taste
Directions:
Preheat oven to 375 degrees and prepare pastry dough according to instructions.

Once dough is thawed, cut into 3x3 squares and place on baking sheet.

Mix ingredients in medium bowl until even. Place mixture inside the center of square.

Join diagonal ends together, making a "purse" shape. If there is possible spillage, secure before placing inside oven.

Cook purses for no more than 20 minutes or until slightly brown.

Broccoli Bites

These great little appetizers are always hit in parties.

Ingredients:

2 medium heads of fresh broccoli, chopped into small pieces

3 eggs, beaten

1 cup of breadcrumbs

1½ cups of low fat cheddar cheese, shredded

Salt and pepper, to taste

Directions:
Preheat oven to 375 degrees F. Grease a baking dish. In a bowl, add all ingredients and mix well. Make small patties with your hands. Place patties on prepared baking dish. Bake for 25 minutes.
Serving Suggestions:
You can enjoy these bites with any sauce of your choice.

Pizza

Eggplant Pizza

Ingredients:

2 large eggplants, sliced as 1-2 inch discs

One cup of marinara or tomato sauce

One tablespoon of garlic, minced or chopped

Two tablespoons of Italian blend seasoning or fresh basil or herbs

One cup of mozzarella cheese, shredded

¼ cup of canola or vegetable oil

Directions:
Preheat oven to 400 degrees. Heat a large skillet on medium and add oil. Add slices and brown on each side for no more than 10 minutes.
Remove and drain discs on paper towel. After a couple of minutes, place discs on baking sheet and top with sauce, followed by cheese and seasoning or herbs.
Bake uncovered for no more than 15 minutes. Let cool for 10 minutes and slice in wedges.

Ginger Pear Pizza

Ingredients:

One loaf of sweet Hawaiian bread

One small can of pears, drained and sliced

One teaspoon of ground ginger

Two teaspoons of brown sugar (any variety)

One cup of ricotta or cream cheese, softened

Directions:

Preheat oven to 400 degrees and slice bread in half horizontally. Place side by side on baking sheet and spread cheese on both halves.

Top with pears, followed by sugar and ginger. Let pizza cook for 15-20 minutes.

Margherita Pizza Bites

Ingredients:

One sheet of lavash bread

One cup of mozzarella cheese, shredded or in one-inch chunks

4-5 Roma tomatoes, sliced horizontally

¼ cup of fresh basil leaves

One tablespoon of olive oil

Directions:
Preheat oven to 400 degrees. Lay bread on baking sheet and top with cheese. Add tomato slices and basil. Drizzle oil across leaves before placing in oven.
Place inside oven and let cook for 20-25 minutes. Let cool for 5 minutes before serving. Cut into desired square size.

Spicy Pita Pizza

Ingredients:

One package of pita bread

One can of tomato sauce

One cup of mozzarella cheese, shredded

One jalapeno, minced

½ cup of sundried tomatoes, chopped

2 teaspoons of Italian blend seasoning

Directions:
Preheat oven to 400 degrees and using a baking sheet, place bread side by side. Spread sauce, followed by cheese and distribute all toppings evenly.
Place inside oven and let cook for about 20 minutes. Let cool and cut into wedges or eat as an entree.

Garden Vegetable Pizza

Ingredients:

2 tablespoons of olive oil

½ cup of zucchini, sliced

½ cup of green bell pepper, cut into 1-inch pieces

½ cup green bell pepper, cut into 1-inch pieces

1 clove of garlic, minced

1 medium onion, sliced

1 (24-ounces) jar of frozen mushroom supreme Italian sauce

2 loaves (1 pound each) of frozen white bread dough, thawed

½ cup of mozzarella cheese, shredded

Directions:
Preheat the oven to 375 degrees F. Grease a 15x10 inch baking pan. In a skillet, heat oil on medium heat. Add zucchini, peppers, garlic and onion. Cook, stirring often till vegetables become tender. Stir in the sauce. Place dough on prepared baking pan, forming a single large crust. Pinch up the edges to form a rim. Spread the vegetable mixture on dough within 1-inch of the edges. Sprinkle cheese on top. Bake for 25 minutes.

Serving Suggestions:
You can enjoy this yummy pizza with mayo garlic dip.

Soups and Salads

Spicy Tomato Celery Soup

Ingredients:

One carton (16 oz) of vegetable broth

One can of tomatoes (chopped)

½ cup of sundried tomatoes (with or without oil)

One cup of celery, chopped 1 inch or less

One teaspoon of crushed red pepper (optional)

One teaspoon of lemon juice

Salt and pepper to taste

Directions:
Heat broth on medium using a medium saucepan, let warm for 5 minutes and add celery. Cover and let sit for 10 minutes.
Mix in both tomatoes and seasonings. Let soup cook for 10-15 minutes and let sit for 30 minutes before serving.

Sweet Potato & Peanut Soup

It's a tasty, balanced and nourishing winter soup which will fill your tummy and keep you warm.

Ingredients:

2 large sweet potatoes, scrubbed and cut in half lengthwise

4 teaspoons of olive oil, divided

1 yellow onion, diced

4 cups of low-sodium vegetable broth

1 cup of canned pineapple, drained and diced

½ jalapeno, seeded

½ cup of creamy salted peanut butter

2 tablespoons of light brown sugar

1 (15-ounce) can of light coconut milk

Salt, to taste

2 tablespoons of fresh cilantro, sliced thinly

4 tablespoons of unsalted peanuts, chopped

Directions:

Preheat oven to 400 degrees F. Line a baking dish with foil. Brush the flesh of sweet potatoes with 2 tablespoons of oil. Place flesh side down in baking dish. Roast for 4o minutes. Scoop out the flesh. In a deep pan, add remaining oil. Add onion and sauté onion for 5 minutes on medium heat. Add cooked potatoes, broth and pineapple. Bring to a boil. Reduce the heat to low. Now, add jalapeno, peanut butter and sugar. Cook for 7 to 8 minutes. Remove from stove. Let it cool for 8 to 10 minutes.

After cooling, add soup in a blender and puree till smooth. Return the pan on low heat. Add coconut milk and salt. Cook, stirring occasionally for 10 minutes or till all ingredients are mixed well. While serving, garnish with cilantro and peanuts.

Serving Suggestions:

Serve this soup with rice and get a full protein meal.

French Onion Soup

Simply outstanding soup.... It will be a great hit for winter dinner.

Ingredients:

2 tablespoons of butter

1 tablespoon of canola oil

1½ pounds of yellow onions, sliced thinly

1 teaspoon of salt

½ teaspoon of sugar

3 tablespoons of flour

6 cups of vegetable broth

1 bay leaf

½ teaspoon of sage powder

2 tablespoons of vinegar

Salt and pepper, to taste

2 tablespoons of cognac

½ raw yellow onion, grated

12 ounces of Swiss cheese, grated

4 ounces of parmesan cheese, grated

8 slices of French bread (1-inch thick), oiled and toasted (in oven for 15 minutes per side)

3 tablespoons of olive oil, for drizzling

Directions:

Heat butter and canola oil in a heavy bottom stock pot on medium-low heat. Stir sliced onion, till coated with oil. Cover and cook till they are translucent and tender on medium-high heat.

Add 1 teaspoon of salt and sugar. Cook, uncovered, stirring frequently till onions are caramelized. Reduce heat to medium-low. Add flour and brown, stirring continuously for 2 to 3 minutes. Add broth, bay leaf, sage and vinegar. Simmer for 30 minutes. Season with salt and pepper if needed. Transfer to a casserole dish. Stir in cognac, grated onion and a few ounces of Swiss cheese. Spread toasted bread with one layer of soup. Sprinkle remaining Swiss and parmesan cheese on bread covering it completely. Drizzle with olive oil. Place in oven at 350 degrees F. Bake for 30 minutes.

Serving Suggestions:

Serve this tasty soup with toasted and buttered rye bread.

Cabbage Soup

Excellent recipe! Delicious and heart warming soup.
Ingredients:

3 tablespoons of butter

1 large onion, chopped

1 celery rib, chopped

1 large carrot, peeled and grated coarsely

1 large head cabbage, shredded

8 cups of vegetable broth

Black peppercorn, to taste

1 bay leaf

2 large russet potatoes, peeled and chopped coarsely

1 (14-ounce) can of diced tomatoes

Salt and pepper, to taste

Sour cream, for garnishing

Fresh dill, for garnishing
Directions:
In a large pan, melt butter and sauté onion till translucent. Add celery, carrot and cabbage. Sauté them, stirring continuously for 3 minutes. Add broth, peppercorn and bay leaf. Bring to a boil. Reduce the heat. Cover and simmer for 15 minutes. Add potatoes and bring to a boil. Reduce heat. Cover and simmer for 10 minutes or till potatoes are tender. Add tomatoes. Bring back

to a boil. Simmer for 5 minutes. Garnish with sour cream and dill before serving.

Serving suggestions:
Enjoy this yummy soup with fresh baguettes.

Cheesy Broccoli Soup

It's a fantastic, yummy and easy to make soup.
Ingredients:

6 tablespoons of butter

1 medium yellow onion, chopped

¼ cup of all-purpose flour

2 cups of milk

3 cups of vegetable broth

Salt and pepper, to taste

Garlic powder, to taste

4 cups of broccoli florets

1 large carrot, sliced (optional)

3 cups of cheddar cheese, grated, plus more for garnishing
Directions:
In a heavy stock pan, add butter and melt on medium heat. Add onion and sauté till tender. Add flour and cook, stirring frequently till it becomes golden. Gradually, add milk, stirring till smooth. Pour chicken broth. Season with salt, pepper and garlic powder. Bring to a boil. Reduce heat to low. Simmer, stirring often for 20 minutes or till thickened. Now add broccoli and carrots (if liked). Simmer for 20 minutes or till tender. Puree the soup in a food processor. Transfer to pot again. Stir in cheese. Garnish with extra cheese while serving.
Serving Suggestions:
If you want this soup extra cheesier then add some Velveeta to thicken.

Almond Bean Salad

Ingredients:

Three cups of fresh string beans, ends removed

½ cup of malt vinegar

One cup of toasted almonds, unsalted

¼ cup of canola or vegetable oil

Salt and pepper to taste

Directions:

Boil or steam beans for no more than 5 minutes total. Let cool in ice water for one minute and drain.

In a large bowl, mix all ingredients together and let chill for about 2 hours before serving.

Extra Lite Potato Salad

Ingredients:

2-3 large Russet potatoes, boiled and chopped

One large cucumber, chopped small

One can of tomatoes, chopped and drained

One red onion, chopped small

One red or orange pepper, chopped small

½ cup of vinegar

One cup of non-fat yogurt

One tablespoon of all-purpose seasoning

Pepper to taste

Directions:
Using a large bowl, add potatoes, followed by vinegar and seasonings. Add remaining vegetables, followed by yogurt.
Mix evenly and serve with meat substitute sandwich

Hot Citrus Bean and Corn Salad

Ingredients:

One 8 oz can of black beans, drained

One 8 oz (or smaller) can of corn, drained

One 8 oz can of tomatoes, drained

½ large onion, chopped fine

½ cup of orange or lemon juice

½ cup of white vinegar

¼ cup of cilantro, chopped fine

Two tsp of crushed red pepper (optional)

Salt and pepper to taste

Directions:
Using a large bowl, mix beans and vegetables evenly, followed by liquids.
Let mixture sit in refrigerator for no less than 2 hours.
Mix in spices and let sit for another hour.
Serve with meatless Latin or Southwest-inspired entrees.

Spicy Corn Salad

Ingredients:

Two cups of frozen corn, thawed; or, one large can of regular corn, drained

One cup of garlic vinegar

One Habanero pepper, chopped

One jalapeno pepper, chopped

One teaspoon of pimentos

½ red onion, chopped fine

Salt and pepper to taste

One teaspoon of agave nectar syrup (optional)
Directions:
Mix all ingredients in a large bowl and let sit in refrigerator for at least 1 hour before serving.

Cucumber & Tomato Salad
It's a refreshing and low calorie but healthy summer salad.
Ingredients:

1 cucumber, deseeded and sliced

1 cup of shallots, sliced

1 cup of grape tomatoes, halved

3 tablespoons of mint, chopped

3 tablespoons of apple cider vinegar

¼ cup of extra virgin olive oil

1 teaspoon of herbs seasoning

Salt and black pepper, to taste
Directions:
In a bowl, mix cucumber, shallots, tomatoes and mint. In another bowl, whisk vinegar, oil, herbs seasoning, salt and black pepper. Pour vinaigrette over salad and toss well.

Serving Suggestions:
This refreshing salad paired nicely with Lebanese kaftas.

Black Beans & Couscous Salad

Enjoy this low fat but very tasty, satisfying and healthy meat alternative salad at lunch.
Ingredients:

1 can of black beans, rinsed

½ large carrot, chopped

2 tablespoons of red onion, chopped

1 green bell pepper, chopped

¼ cup of fresh cilantro, chopped roughly

½ fresh jalapeño, removed membrane and seeds, and minced

1 cup of whole wheat couscous, cooked (according to package directions)

1 tablespoon of extra virgin olive oil

Juice of 1 lime

1 teaspoon of vinegar

1 teaspoon of cumin powder

¼ teaspoon of onion salt

Black pepper, to taste

A pinch of salt
Directions:

In a bowl, mix beans, carrot, onion, bell pepper, cilantro and jalapeño. Add couscous, oil, lime juice vinegar and toss well. Add seasoning and mix well.

Serving Suggestions:

You can enjoy this healthy salad with main course veggie meals.

Fruit Dishes

Apple Cranberry Sauce

Ingredients:

2-3 apples, chopped

One cup of cranberries, fresh or frozen

Two cups of apple juice

One teaspoon of ginger, ground

½ teaspoon of cinnamon

One teaspoon of vanilla extract

½ cup of walnut halves (optional)

Directions:

Heat a large saucepan on medium and add juice. When brought to a boil, add fruits and let simmer for about 20 minutes.

Mix in spices and cover; remove from heat and let sit for no more than 20 minutes.

Serve with cottage cheese or yogurt.

Baked apples

Ingredients:

4-6 apples, sliced in halves and cored

1 cup of apple juice

One teaspoon of cinnamon, ginger or apple pie spice

One tablespoon of margarine (optional)
Directions:
Preheat oven on broil. On a baking sheet, place apple halves side-by-side. Pour juice inside each middle, followed by spices. Cook for about 15-20 minutes until brown. Coat inside with a light spread of margarine and let cook an additional 5 minutes. Eat alone or add a dollop of vanilla non-fat yogurt or cottage cheese.

Watermelon Salsa

Really a GEM of recipe! It's an easy to make, crunchy and delicious dish for parties.
Ingredients:

2 cups of watermelon, seeded and chopped finely

1 cup of sweet onion, minced

1 cup of crushed pineapple, drained

¼ cup of orange juice

¼ cup of fresh cilantro, chopped

1/4 teaspoon of Tabasco sauce

Directions:
Mix all ingredients in a bowl and stir well. Cover and refrigerate for 30 minutes before serving.

Try this crunchy salsa with tortilla chips and have great taste.

Apple Chutney

Wonderful chutney! This is a perfect blend of apples and spices.
Ingredients:

2 cups of sugar

2 cups of apple cider vinegar

3 tablespoons of fresh lemon juice

1½ pounds of tart green apples, peeled, cored and chopped (½-inch pieces)

1½ teaspoon of salt

1 teaspoon of crushed red peppers

12-ounces piece of fresh ginger, peeled and chopped coarsely

10 large cloves of garlic

2 tablespoons of yellow mustard seeds

1½ cups of (packed) golden raisin
Directions:
In a heavy large pan, add sugar and vinegar. Bring to a boil. Cook, stirring till sugar dissolves. Reduce heat. Simmer for 10 minutes. Remove from stove. In a large bowl, add lemon juice and apples and toss well. Blend salt, red pepper, ginger and garlic in a food processor. Blend till chopped finely. Add apples, garlic mixture, mustard seeds and raisins into vinegar. Simmer, stirring often for 45 minutes or till chutney thickens. Pour into a bowl. Cover and chill.

This delicious chutney would go well with grilled cheese sandwich.

Apple & Banana Quesadilla

Make these yummy and nutrient sandwiches for your kid's lunchbox and surely they will love it.

Ingredients:

1 apple, peeled and cut into chunks

1 banana, sliced into thin rounds

¼ teaspoon of brown sugar

½ teaspoon of nutmeg powder

¼ teaspoon of cinnamon powder

¾ cup of peanut butter

8 slices of whole wheat bread

Cooking spray

Directions:
Puree apple in a food processor till small in size. Puree banana also. Mix apple and banana. Stir in all spices and peanut butter till mixed completely. Spread filling evenly between sandwiches. Spray a non stick frying pan. Heat frying pan on medium heat. Grill sandwiches over pan for about 3 minutes per side.

Serving Suggestions:
Enjoy these sandwiches with fruit salsa and vanilla yogurt.

Rice Dishes

Cajun Rice

Ingredients:

Two cups of instant rice (brown or white)

One can of mushroom soup, creamed

One teaspoon of agave nectar syrup

One jalapeno, chopped fine

Two tablespoons of Cajun seasoning

One teaspoon of margarine or butter

One cup of water

Directions:
In a large pan, heat water until boiling and add rice. Mix in soup, peppers, butter and seasonings while on medium heat. Cook for about 10 minutes and cover. Remove from heat.
Let sit for 30 minutes, stirring every 10 minutes.

Vegetarian Rice Bake

Ingredients:

Two cups of instant rice

One can of tomatoes, chopped or stewed

One cup of frozen spinach, chopped and thawed

One cup of mushrooms, sliced

One bell pepper, chopped

½ onion, chopped

½ cup of all purpose seasoning

Pepper to taste

One cup of cheddar or jack cheese, shredded

½ cup of bread crumbs (optional)

Directions:
Preheat oven to 350 degrees. In a casserole dish, add vegetables, followed by rice. Mix thoroughly and add spices.
Cover and place in oven for 30-40 minutes.
Remove and top with cheese and bread crumbs. Cook until brown.

Carrot & Pea Rice Pilaf

A classic rice dish! Guaranteed to please the family and make them say please give me more.

Ingredients:

3 tablespoons of butter

2 medium carrots, diced

2 cups of long-grain white rice

1 (14-ounces) can of vegetable broth

Salt and black pepper, to taste

1 small bay leaf

2 medium scallions, sliced

1 (10-ounces) can of frozen peas

Directions:
Melt butter in a large pan on medium heat. Add carrots and cook, stirring often for 2 to 3 minutes. Add rice and cook, stirring till rice is well coated. Add broth, salt, pepper, bay leaf and 2 cups of water. Bring to a boil on high heat. Reduce heat to low. Cover and simmer for 15 to 20 minutes or till rice is tender and all liquid is absorbed. Now stir in scallion and peas. Heat it completely.

Serving Suggestions:
Serve this rice dish along with fresh tomato cooler.

Spicy Beans & Rice

Perfect and yummy meal! Surely you will add this recipe in your weekly menu list.

Ingredients:

2 tablespoons of olive oil

4 cloves of garlic, minced

1 medium onion, chopped

½ cup of salsa

1 (14 ½ ounces) can of Mexican-style stewed tomatoes, undrained

1 (15-ounce) can of black beans, drained

Salt, to taste

Cayenne pepper, to taste

2 cups of long grain rice, cooked (hot)

½ cup of cheddar cheese, shredded

Directions:
In a medium pan, add oil and heat on medium heat. Add garlic and onion and sauté till tender. Stir in salsa, tomatoes, beans, salt and pepper. Bring to a boil. Reduce heat to medium-low. Simmer for 15 minutes. Mix rice in beans mixture just before serving. Garnish with shredded cheese.

Serving Suggestions:
Enhance the flavor of spiced rice by serving with avocado salsa.

Squash Risotto

You will love this creamy, colorful and flavored rice dish with little sweet texture of butternut squash.
Ingredients:

5½ cups of low-sodium vegetable broth

1 tablespoon of canola oil

1 medium onion, chopped finely

1½ cups of Arborio rice

1¼ cups of frozen butternut squash puree, thawed

½ cup of Parmesan cheese, shredded, divided

2 tablespoons of fresh sage, chopped

Salt and black pepper, to taste
Directions:
Add broth in a pan and heat it till hot but not boiling. Reduce heat to very low. Cover to keep warm. Heat olive oil in a large pan on medium heat. Add onion and stir for 6 to 7 minutes till softened. Add onion and stir for 1 minute. Add warm broth and cook for about 30 minutes or till rice are tender and all broth is absorbed. Now, add squash puree, half of cheese, sage, salt and black pepper and mix. Garnish with remaining cheese while serving.
Serving Suggestions:
Increase the flavor of this wonderful dish by sprinkling roasted pine nuts and balsamic glaze.

Vegetarian Dishes

Carrot Ginger Stew

Ingredients:

5-6 carrots, peeled and chopped to 1 inch thick

2-3 parsnips, peeled and chopped to 1 inch thick

One packet of instant mashed potatoes or one large baked potato

¼ pound of fresh ginger root, peeled and chopped or minced

½ cup of honey

One cup of orange juice

One tablespoon of garlic powder

Salt and pepper to taste

Four cups of water

Directions:
Using a large, covered pan or Dutch oven, boil the ginger root in water for about 20 minutes. Remove excess pieces and add carrots and parsnips and cook for 20 minutes.

Place about half of cooked vegetables in a separate bowl and mash remainder until fairly smooth. Add potatoes and water, as needed and stir until smooth in texture.

Remove from heat and add juice, vegetables, seasonings and honey. Mix well, cover and let sit for about 45 minutes, stirring every few minutes.

Garlic Pepper Beans

Ingredients:

One pound of fresh green beans, with ends removed

One large red, orange or yellow pepper, sliced lengthwise

One tablespoon of garlic, minced

Sea salt and ground pepper to taste

One tablespoon of Canola or sesame oil

Directions:
Heat the oil on medium heat using a large, covered pan. Rinse beans, pat dry and add to pan, followed by pepper slices.
Saute for 5 minutes, ensuring that vegetable are coated evenly.
Mix in garlic, seasonings and cover. Remove from heat and let sit for 15-20 minutes.
Serve with grain or pasta entree

Spinach Patties

Ingredients:

Two cups of bread, any variety, crumbled

One cup of spinach

One can of mushroom soup, creamed

½ onion, chopped fine

½ cup of imitation bacon (optional)

½ cup of Swiss cheese, shredded or chopped small

One tablespoon of all purpose seasoning

Pepper to taste

One cup of canola oil

Directions:
Using a large bowl, mix bread and vegetables evenly, followed by soup. Add seasonings, cheese and bacon.

Heat the oil on medium inside large pan and form balls that fit in palm of hand.

Place each ball carefully in oil and press down lightly to flatten. Let brown on one side before turning. Turn heat to low and let other side cook for at least 10 minutes.

Drain patties on paper towel and serve with salad.

Lime Orzo Stew

Colorful vegetables and the flavor of lime and Italian seasoning make this orzo dish a great treat for eyes and tongue.

Ingredients:

2 tablespoons of olive oil

2 cups of orzo pasta

2 cloves of garlic, minced

1 carrot, peeled and shredded

1 zucchini, peeled and shredded

1 (14-ounces) can of vegetable broth

1 teaspoon of dry basil leaves

1 (16-ounce) can of stewed tomatoes, undrained

1 teaspoon of Italian seasoning

Salt and pepper, to taste

2 teaspoons of lime juice

2 teaspoons of lime zest, grated

2 teaspoons of fresh parsley, chopped

¼ cup of scallions, chopped

½ cup of parmesan cheese, grated

Directions:
Add oil in a large pan and heat on medium-high heat. Add orzo and garlic. Cook, stirring for 5 minutes or till pasta changes into a light golden color. Add carrots and zucchini. Cook for 2 minutes or till vegetables become soften. Add broth, basil, tomatoes, Italian seasoning, salt and pepper. Bring to a boil. Reduce heat to medium. Cover and simmer for 10 minutes or till all liquid is absorbed. Stir in lime juice, lime zest, parsley and scallions. Remove from stove. Garnish with cheese while serving.

Serving Suggestions:
You can sprinkle some roasted nuts like walnut, peanut or almonds to enhance the flavor.

Black Bean Burgers

Incredible Bean burger would make a tasty, healthy and good lunch meal.
Ingredients:
For Burger Patties:

2 (15-ounces) cans of black beans, rinsed and drained

½ cup of canned corn kernels, drained

1 jalapeno, removed seeds

1 tablespoon of onion, chopped finely

2 scallions, chopped finely

3 tablespoons of tomato paste

Hot sauce, to taste

Salt and black pepper, to taste

½ teaspoon of cumin powder

½ teaspoon of garlic powder

2 eggs

½ cup of bread crumbs
For Creamy Mayo:

2 teaspoons of creamy horseradish sauce

½ cup mayonnaise

Hot sauce, to taste
For Burgers:

6 hamburger buns

Butter

6 slices of cheddar cheese

Lettuce leaves

Tomato slices

Red onion rings

Directions:

Add beans in a large bowl and mash with a potato masher till ¾ of beans are smashed. Add all ingredients and mix well till mixture blends together. Make six patties from the mixture. Heat a non-stick frying pan on medium heat. Drizzle with some olive oil in pan. Cook patties for 4 to 5 minutes each side. Now add cheese slices on top of patties. Cover with foil to keep warm.

Stir together horseradish cream, mayonnaise and hot sauce till smooth.

Butter each side of buns. Grill the buns on heated pan. Spread horseradish mayo from each side of buns. Place a Pattie on bun. Top with lettuce, tomato slices and onion rings.

Serving Suggestions:
Enjoy these yummy burgers with French fries and Cole slaw.